8 Decisions Every

Man Should Make

A STUDY OF THE EIGHT PEOPLE INSIDE OF YOU THAT DETERMINE WHO YOU ARE

Jeff Miller

ISBN 13: 978-1-7904-0220-5

CONTENTS

ACKNOWLEDGMENTS

I wish to recognize four inspirations for the content of this writing.

First, there are four men who have shaped my life significantly. Some are still alive, some are dead. These men fathered me, taught me, gave me chances, believed in me, hurt me deeply, deserted me, and stuck with me. Through deep joy and pain I have learned much from each of them. In our youth we look to older men to lead and nourish us through love and affirmation; as we age we realize that we can be led and nourished just as much, if not more so, through their wounding (for they are imperfect). Profound thanks goes to these men, unnamed, who have sown deeply into my soul.

Second, there are scores of men I call brothers who have walked this journey with me over the last many years. I have spent thousands of hours with these men over coffee, campfires, and hiking trails. We have laughed together and we have cried together - these are the things of brotherhood. As the book of Proverbs says, "there is a friend who sticks closer than a brother,"[1] and I am privileged to have found many of these friends in my life.

Third, I have learned much from the works of so many who I will quote in this book. These ideas are not original, but rather a compilation and distillation of many insights using my voice and mind to explain what I have and am still learning. There is an abundance of material on archetypes found in psychology and classic fiction literature. I encourage anyone reading this to explore my referenced writings further.

Finally, I wish to thank my wife Jennifer for her support of this work. There are not words to describe how exceptional a person she is, so I will not make the attempt.

I would also like to acknowledge and thank my friends Nick D'Acquisto, Isaac Goff, and Sarah Darr, along with my friend and older brother Thomas Miller. These served as editors to this work; it reads better because of their input. Also thank you to those who gave of their resources to assist in funding the publication of this book; again, the final product is better because of the generosity of others.

INTRODUCTION

HOW TO READ A BOOK

I assume that you aim to read, not skim, this book. On my part, each syllable of each word has thought and life behind it, and in writing this book I intend it to be transformative for the reader. These days books are rushed through almost as quickly as they were thrown into fires in Ray Bradbury's fantastic work *Fahrenheit 451*. There is an over-availability of information, much of it baseless, in our culture; this has produced many a "reader" that cannot read things. "Oh, I read that." No, you did not. You bought it in response to a flame that burned briefly within you, but you never tended that flame. It has gone out and the book that you purchased, whether digitally or in real life, is in a file or stack with dozens of others, collecting dust.

Books on screens are often not finished and quickly forgotten, maybe more so than printed books due to their more-easily-disposable nature. Click and forget. I prefer the smell of paper, the ability to underline and mark up and color with a pen or pencil (yes, all these can be done electronically; bear with me), and the nostalgia of a worn copy of an oft-read book. A physical library does something to an office. A physical book is a visceral experience, especially if used. Books are not a commodity; they should be treasured, the favorites read and re-read. Good books are a joy to receive and to give away.

Years ago in university I read hundreds of books. Later, I resolved to enroll myself in proverbial graduate school in the sense that I would read for all of my life, ever educating myself. In the last few decades, some books were given to me, others I heard about or learned about in a footnote and sought out myself. In one way or another these books have appeared in my life. In my younger years I would typically have six or eight books I was reading at once. At some point that number dwindled to two or three, and these days I only read the books I know are the right ones for me. I do so very slowly and thoughtfully, taking notes, underlining, and journaling about what I have learned once finished.

All that is to say: Take it slow. Most authors got into writing a book or books because there was some deep thing in them that they wished to convey to others. I am no exception. You cannot expect to understand deep things by a quick and shallow reading of a book. This is not a book to blast through in one week. Let each chapter sit with you for a while, let your life marinate in what you read, and vice-versa. Interact with it, extract what is good for your soul, then move on.

ABOUT THIS BOOK
8 Decisions Every Man Should Make is a study of eight different personalities that exist, some more prominently than others, in each man. These classic archetypes are found in many other formats in many other books. Myths and stories throughout the history of mankind in all cultures contain well defined themes, characters, and roles that appear over and over. For example, Hercules is a Fighter, as are Indiana Jones and The Man in Black. Yoda is a Wizard,

as are John the Baptist and Morpheus. Through the millennia, the same story is told and re-told; man is presented to us as all he can be in his many facets.

This book is another interpretation of the composition of a man's soul as seen through my particular lens. The eight archetypes I choose to discuss are: King, Lover, Fighter, Jester, Artist, Mourner, Wizard, and Mystic. These eight types all come together to form the core of a man, and they determine much of what his life will look like.

As we consider the ingredients of the psyche of a man, this particular reading differs from others in that we will study manhood from a more diverse and holistic approach. Most books about men readily acknowledge the presence of the Fighter and the Lover. But tapping into the Jester or the Mystic might seem more abstract. One generation, geography, or context will naturally emphasize certain aspects of manhood to the exclusion of others; this writing is an attempt to examine the bare soul and potential of manhood from an angle that captures a truly all-inclusive picture. We look from a perspective that affirms the physical, mental, emotional, and spiritual experiences and expressions of the male soul.

The title I have chosen, *8 Decisions Every Man Should Make*, is an intentional challenge to the reader to embrace each of these facets of manhood. The book at its core is actually more of a study of these eight archetypes, but the very act of digesting the material should evoke some level of conviction in any man that has a pulse. There are choices to be made, and those choices determine what kind of man we will become. The very nature of this study then tasks the reader to apply what is being learned and make some decisions. Hence the title.

Each of these eight types is described in a chapter all its own. All men are on a journey to achieve maturity in each. A man's particular temperament, upbringing, life experiences, and choices all contribute to the development of each personality in him. Ideally all eight would co-exist in their "prime" or original form in a healthy male. However, for each archetype, there are two imposters who can take over and distort the potential that a man is capable of achieving. One represents the underdevelopment of said archetype, and the other epitomizes its overdevelopment.

For example, let us discuss the Fighter in brief. The Fighter's purpose is to battle. A wise man will learn how to fight, when it is right to fight, and which battles are not worth fighting. He will stand up for a cause and defend it at the cost of his health, reputation, and possibly even his life. This takes courage, strength, and conviction. However, there are two imposters that may take the place of the Fighter in a man. The underdevelopment of the Fighter results in him being replaced by the Coward. The Coward has no great cause and will choose not to fight for anything, resulting in a man who is weak, impressionable, and flaccid. Just as dangerous is the overdevelopment of the Fighter which results in him metamorphosing into the Brute. The Brute is a beast who finds his identity in fighting. He will fight for anything or for nothing. He fights to win whether or not what he has won is worth winning and regardless of the cost to the loser. He knows little of nobility nor restraint.

So it is: there are eight archetypes and sixteen distortions of these, one the under- and the other the over-emphasis of its true and right nature. That means there are twenty-four different personalities competing for influence in the soul of a man, but only room for eight of them. Using this grid as a reference, it is very easy to see how many varieties of men there are. One might be very balanced in the Wizard (the teachable student) persona, but the Coward has replaced their Fighter and the Fool has replaced their Jester. The possibilities of different soul compositions, according to this model and a bit of simple math, is 6561. In short, using this paradigm for personality inclination and soul development, there are thousands of possible types of men we can become.

It is a given that you or I might naturally emphasize a few of these persons more strongly than others, while another man might embody still different ones. Part of that is simply who we were created to be. I might be very much a Lover but very little an Artist, and that is okay. The important thing is that the Artist in me is alive and healthy, even if it is taking a smaller role in my life when compared to the man next to me.

In these pages the reader is given the opportunity to study each archetype and to also study himself to discern whether he is in or out of balance. The eight decisions to be made are simply to choose the healthy archetype instead of the two unhealthy alternatives presented. These are not one-time decisions, but life-long commitments to choosing health and balance. It is my hope that, to that end, this book serves as both a mirror and a lighthouse.

At the end of each chapter you will find a call to decision-making along with homework - a study guide of sorts. A book like this could be studied together very easily in 10-12 weekly meetings where the participants read a chapter before each meeting and then gather to have discussion. Confession, building of trust, and self-awareness can lead to immense healing as these issues are shared with maturity and brotherhood as the goal. Whether reading alone or with others, the opportunity is before the reader to look at himself and invite change to take place if needed.

As we wrap up our study in the final chapter, I will conclude with some practical things that can be done to move towards health. These will be more "big picture" and will apply to all eight archetypes. They are things we can proactively do that will position us in a place to grow.

In the appendix, along with notes and references, you will find a section titled "At a Glance." This is a quick guide to the qualities of the twenty-four people described in this book and can be used as an orientation or tool for self-evaluation. Use this now or later to perhaps get an idea of where you might stand as a man. This reference is a simple way to get started, to see the "YOU ARE HERE" as on a building schematic and therefore have an understanding of where to go next.

Obviously, in different seasons of life we are different people. The journey to healthy masculinity is never-ending, and we will always be striving for balance in these areas. In some areas you will find that you are balanced and healthy, while in others you will find room for improvement. A year from now, things might look very different in your life and therefore your struggles and successes as they relate to this material might take a different form.

My goal is that you the reader will come to know yourself more in these pages - that you will find joy in celebrating your strengths and be spurred to grow in the areas where you can improve. I challenge you to make these eight decisions. Embrace the best that you can be, and in turn leave behind patterns and dysfunction that are handicapping your ability to be a man.

The road to manhood. It is fraught with difficulty and discovery; with blood, sweat, and tears - and then more blood, sweat, and tears. Many reject this path, but some embark on it, carrying their guts behind them. It is a hard journey, a way less traveled, but one that is very much worth it. I invite you to join me in this adventure.

The King

"For this is what it means to be a king: to be first in every desperate attack and last in every desperate retreat, and when there's hunger in the land (as must be now and then in bad years) to wear finer clothes and laugh louder over a scantier meal than any man in your land." [1]
– C. S. Lewis

Purpose: *To lead.*

Decision: *To courageously lead some great cause in a way that others can follow.*

In every man there is a King. This person inspires those around him to be better than they are and to go places they do not feel capable of going. He knows the next step, and he can help others take it with a sense of hope. He is the one people look to when the unexpected happens. He is the least anxious person in the room. The King will bravely guide us into the unknown, and then bring us out alive.

KINGS ARE KNOWN FOR SOMETHING

Finding Kings throughout human history, myth, and fiction is not hard. A pioneer like George Washington, a trailblazer like William Wallace - these are kingly leaders. Jason led the Argonauts, King David led the armies of Israel. These are heroes; men of renown of whom the world is not worthy. They left their mark, both on their physical world and in our hearts through the power of legend and story.

While a man may not become famous as these did, because of the King in him he will stand out and be known for something. He stands for some great cause, and his commitment to it brings followers, respect, criticism, and fame, whether on a large or small scale. People are attracted to someone who knows what they are about. When a King walks into a room, anyone who knows him at all is aware that he stands for something.

THE KING SETS THE TONE IN A ROOM

A King has tremendous influence in the arena in which he operates, and because of this, he can be a source of strength to those around him. A husband, accepting his role as King, will humbly but bravely lead his marriage. A father, if the King is alive in him, will create a hopeful atmosphere in his household. People feel safe in the presence of a good King because that presence evokes safety and courage, as if something good is going to happen within or under his reign.

Kings have a certain composure about them that can have a powerful effect on anyone nearby. They carry a strength and dignity about them. When a King is present, difficult circumstances do not bear upon us as they might if we were alone. Perhaps you know nothing about automobile repair, and when your car leaves you stranded you have a certain sense of anxiety. Your friend shows up to help, a skilled mechanic with the heart of a King, and in short time the car is running again. Or perhaps a loved one becomes seriously ill. There is despair in the waiting room at the hospital, but when a King walks in, perhaps in the form of a chaplain or clergyman, things seem less grave than they were before.

THE KING KNOWS WHAT HE'S ABOUT

When the King is in charge a man knows why he wakes up in the morning and what he is to be about. He has seen many causes, some small and some great, some unworthy and some very worthy, and has purposed to point his life toward fulfilling ones that he is passionate about. His sureness of this cause and his commitment to it create a nobility in him that rises above what others think of it, whether or not they are supportive.

Robert Bly cements this idea in his excellent book *Iron John*: "The inner king is the one in us who knows what we want to be for the rest of our lives, or the rest of the month, or the rest of the day. He can make clear what we want without being contaminated in his choice by the opinions of others around us. The inner king is connected with our fire and purpose and passion."[2]

KINGS ARE PRESENT AT REGAL MOMENTS

Real-life kings hold judicial court; they approve laws, appoint and promote, and remove troublemakers. They attend festivals, give speeches, and lead battles. They are the highlight of the parade and proudly display their queen, princes, and princesses.

In like manner, the man who is a King prioritizes important events and milestones. He remembers his anniversary, trims his facial hair, and dons his best clothing. He celebrates his children; he is the cornerstone of important initiatory events in their lives, especially his sons. From him they learn to swing a hammer, drive a car, bleed without crying, date the right person, and treat a woman the right way. He champions the well-being of the people in his life. He is always present at the crossroads in their journeys, encouraging them on.

THE KING LEADS IN A WAY THAT OTHERS CAN FOLLOW

When a King leads, he does so with courage, but this courage is balanced with care. He understands that if others cannot embrace his vision, he may be realizing it by himself. In order to make it possible for others to follow, he leads as a servant, with grace for others that need tutoring along the way.

Once on a mountain hike with about a dozen friends one of my then-adolescent sons blazed ahead of the group, skipping along the boulder-laden incline like a mountain gazelle. He took the right kind of pride in his teenage strength, his long legs effortlessly propelling him quickly ahead of the rest of the party. Excited to lead the group up the mountain and prove it could be done, he progressed so quickly that we nearly lost sight of him, as only a few among the group could keep up.

Before he left everyone completely behind, I caught up with him and we had a memorable talk about what it means to be a leader. "You're only a leader if they're able to follow!" I told him. We discussed the privilege of being the point man, of blazing the trail, and the inherent responsibility to serve and lead people in a way that they were able to follow. He slowed down, corralled our group onward and upward, and learned a valuable lesson.

THE KING DOES NOT HAVE TO BE FIRST

As we have said, the King is a leader. He might not be the recognized leader in any given setting, but he exudes leadership nonetheless. This might evidence itself by serving others, by taking the last place at the table, or by withholding speech in a debate, but it is nonetheless leading. The King sees what is needed at the moment, whether it be sound or silence, and acts accordingly. His choices are not dependent on what the majority would do, but instead on what is right.

There is a moving chase scene in George Miller's brilliant film *Mad Max: Fury Road* where the protagonist, Max, demonstrates this beautifully. Their vehicle stuck in the mud, the heroes have nowhere to go as the crazed Bullet Farmer closes in on them, guns blazing. Max has a rifle but only has three shots, two of which he fires as his enemy comes nearer and nearer. The tension swells as he misses both. Just as he prepares to fire the last bullet, his final chance to avoid certain death, he pauses. Behind him stands Furiosa, who he knows to be a better shot than he is. Expressionless, he hands her the gun, allows her to use his shoulder as a prop, and the day is saved.[3]

A healthy and balanced King allows a man to not only lead by leading, but also by deferring to others, by giving away leadership, and by taking the role of servant. A King recognizes that even he has a greater authority in his life, and because of this he can follow or defer to others when the situation dictates. He understands the relationship between his being under authority and his wielding of the same, and because of this he can lead with humility.

YOU DON'T NEED A CROWN TO BE A KING

Not all Kings have crowns, and some men wear crowns but are not Kings. A man can exhibit regality anywhere; perhaps this is one of the truest tests of kingship. The pageantry and scepter are not always necessary.

I have a friend who is a plumber. He works alone and he is a master at his trade. I have watched him at work many times, and he always stands out. Not only does he move three times as fast as everyone else around him, but his craftsmanship when plumbing new construction is like artwork. Everything is straight and clean; there are no corners cut. He may be laying pipe to carry human waste, but he does so like a King.

Two of my three sons happened to find their first employment at McDonald's. These were high school jobs that served the purpose of funding their first automobile purchase, the necessary gas and insurance, and the beginnings of a savings account. Work of the more demeaning nature is good for a boy who is becoming a man. There are many lessons to be learned. Before they were of driving age, I was their chauffeur to and from work, which lent to many opportunities for conversation on the way home. How was the night? What are your co-workers like? What burger sells the most? How many Cokes did you guzzle tonight?

Often, we talked about work ethic and the very low standards of the employees and even managers at their place of employment. Going to work in an environment where nobody cares is difficult. I taught my boys that whether they were flying an airplane or flipping a hamburger, they could do either with excellence, and how they did the latter might have something to do with how they one day would do the former (or whatever field they ended up in). You can earn minimum wage and still be a King.

A KING DOES NOT NEED TO BE NEEDED BY THOSE FOLLOWING HIM

A King does not lead for the sake of the loyalty of his followers, but rather in spite of it. This may seem cold and unfeeling, but it is a key principle of leadership. A sinister codependency often exists among a leader and the people he is leading – a boss and his staff, a pastor and his congregation, a coach and his team.

Those who would presume to lead must understand this, that the leader is the leader because he is the leader, period. Without arrogance he must accept his role and responsibility to lead well and accomplish his objective. The people he is leading will, often without knowing they are doing it, attempt a passive-aggressive coup d'état. This is demonstrated by the outspoken board member on a committee, by the self-focused child covertly trying to get more dessert, by the peremptory woman in the back of the sanctuary that controls the church with her eyeballs. The King is able to politely (or not) ignore such takeover attempts because he does not identify himself by the fickle loyalty of his followers, but rather by the integrity of his leadership and his commitment to his calling.

We find interesting commentary on Jesus the Nazarene in this regard in the second chapter of the Gospel of John. Despite his followers having supposedly "believed in his name" one sentence earlier, we are told that Jesus did not entrust himself to them because he knew what was in man, what man was capable of.[4] He had no faith in their faith, and he did not need their loyalty to validate himself. This made him free to fulfill his calling without it being attached to the approval of others.

KINGS HAVE KNIVES STICKING OUT OF THEIR BACKS

Kings have critics, and being a King means that you will always be a target. This is a hard truth that must be accepted without spite or bitterness. That is to say, it would be very easy for someone who courageously stands up in a crowd to then pine at the fact that everyone else can now notice him, that some will choose to offer their unhelpful commentary, as if this was not part of what it means to lead. A King that complains about his followers often will not be a King for long.

The King is often misunderstood, and he must guard against identifying too much with this reality. Many men who become Kings lose their kingship before long because instead of accepting their job description, which includes criticism and opposition, they grow weary of tolerating the same and go either into hiding or on the warpath. One of the inescapable costs of being King is that we will become front page news, the stories often written by our opponents. A man who wishes to be a King must accept this and not let it bother him too much.

Kings will often experience loneliness because they must make decisions that few will appreciate. The King does this because he sees the big picture and functions according to principles that may not make sense to others. He is in a position that offers a perspective that others do not understand, and he must have the mettle to think and act despite their disapproval.

When acting as a King a man is sure to be villainized by others; as he grows in wisdom he will anticipate this and learn to not defend himself because he knows that others will not understand his viewpoint. As the old Indian proverb says, "Do not judge your brother until you have walked a mile in his moccasins." The seasoned King is humbly content having travelled that mile ahead of everyone else, and without playing the role of victim at their criticism, holds to his vision in the midst of it.

THE KING ABSORBS THE STRESS OF OTHERS

While the King may be criticized and perceived as an unfeeling dictator because of some of the qualities above, it is ironic that he is also perceived as the pillar that holds under pressure, the glue that holds things together. This is because a King has the ability to stoically absorb costs and consequences that others incur and create. There is nobody else to do so; by default and because of the role he is in, the King must accept this. It is the parent, not the child, that cleans up the broken glass or pays for the cracked window. It is the teacher, not the student, who works extra hours to help students who are failing. It is the priest, not the confessor, who spends hours listening to and bearing the problems of others.

A King presents himself with a steely composure. Suppose you were in an elevator or a room filled with people and suddenly the power and lights went out. The majority of the people in the room would likely begin to talk, cry out, or gasp in bewilderment and fear. The King in the room is the man who does not move and says nothing.

KINGS HAVE A BROAD PERSPECTIVE ON LIFE

A King is able to maintain this type of fortitude because it is a reflection of the peace inside of him that navigates his speech and actions. A man who is a King has weathered many battles and achievements, and because of this he is able to understand life from a place of trust and experience.

A man of this nature can endure a sleepless night without complaining because he has in the past endured two sleepless nights and survived. As a father, he is not surprised when other children misbehave because he has experienced the tantrums of a two-year-old already. He does not give up and fall into a mood when he has a fight with his wife because he knows a better day will come. He understands that, as it applies to all of life, he will never be completely fixed and he will never be completely broken. From this place of resolve he lives his life as someone who is not startled when the washing machine breaks or when a cockroach crawls across the kitchen floor during dinner.

One of my first classes in the school of leadership was managing a failing department at the local shopping mall.

When offered this position, I was the youngest person on the team and carried the least amount of seniority. I got the job because I worked harder than the other twenty-four people on the crew and because I expressed interest in advancement. Being promoted meant my salary doubled instantly - but my troubles had just begun.

My new kingdom, as it were, was in big trouble. There was a small group of employees who had been there, it seemed, since time began. They were pretty much calling all the shots, and they weren't calling them well. Things were messy, disorganized, and inefficient. My department was the laughingstock of the entire store. Among my crew were people stealing televisions, sleeping while on the clock, and working with such negligence that it made double work for me.

I spent the next eighteen months trying to create order from chaos, which meant firing a third of the staff and completely reorganizing how things were done. This led to exhaustion, constant conflict, and a death threat from one disgruntled person whom I fired. But I had a lifeline: My boss who coached me through this period was an accomplished King himself, and he believed in me.

During my yearly performance review, in the thick of that difficult year and a half, his advice to me was this: "Jeff, you're very nice to your people, but you don't have teeth. You need teeth. Making your department better is going to mean laying down the law and making some people angry with you, but it's necessary if you want to get your job done. You have to care enough to be tough."

I did what he said – rather than simply working harder (which was my default strategy), I got rid of the rabble, cleaned things up, and acted like a leader. Within a year the department became one of the best performing in the store, and I grew immensely in my understanding of what it meant to be a King.

When a man is fulfilling his role as King, many great things happen. He stands for a worthy cause and leads others in the same direction. The people around him benefit as a result.

But for the man that does not take the lonely and often difficult road of being King, there are two substitutes that lurk in the shadows of his soul, ready to assume control. An under-emphasis of kingly leadership in a man causes him to surrender the reins to the Abdicator, while an over-emphasis of the same results in the dictatorship of the Mogul.

THE ABDICATOR

When a man neglects the role of King in his life, the Abdicator assumes control.

The Abdicator is famous for many accepted behaviors today. He passes the buck, plays the victim, and moves out of the way. When a challenge presents itself, his default is to "let someone else do it." The inconvenience of getting his hands dirty in order to make a situation right is the arbiter in his life, resulting in a limp, soft personality. When he presents his opinion, the Abdicator speaks with an interrogative inflection in his voice, in order that all hearers will have been forewarned with a disclaimer in the event that they do not necessarily agree with his statements.

The Abdicator lives for the approval of others. Often, he chooses not to lead because of the work involved in combating another person's opinion or direction. Rather than disappoint or contend with someone else, he chooses instead to do nothing and become a follower. He might do this at his workplace, in his marriage, or even with his children. Many men give way to the Abdicator when their children turn twelve or thirteen, but some do so when they reach age two.

Our modern culture is filled with famous Abdicators whose behavior is a source of amusement for others. A prime example of this is the bumbling dupe presented to us in the character of Homer Simpson. This man captured the admiration of an entire generation and told them that it was okay to be an idiot and stand for nothing.

Rather than take the hard road of Kingship, the Abdicator remains on the couch, hemming and hawing about how tired he is and how he has no energy left for this or that. He is content to let the world exist around him as it would without his input, so long as he can relax and not be too bothered by anything. When he is, the collective abdication pent up inside of him explodes, fierce threats are unleashed, but within five minutes he settles down over a microwave pizza or something else that will placate his sense of urgency.

This passive attitude causes the Abdicator to be absent and "check out" often. He might have fathered children that do not know who he even is or if he is still alive. If he is present in his children's lives, he misses birthday parties. His wife takes his children to obligations and social events, perhaps to church, and is viewed as "wearing the pants in the family." The children might even unknowingly default to going to mom for everything because they have learned that she has the answers whereas dad will simply send them to mother. Why go through the middle man? The Abdicator has unconsciously planned things this way in order to save him from the inconvenience of responsibility.

For many men, the management of the Abdicator over their soul is the result of having no model for leadership in their life. The amount of men without a father in our times is staggering. While different men respond to this in different ways, many choose the role of abdicating. For them it is easier to remain uninvolved in the gridlock of relationships, great causes, and stress.

For example, while allocating a portion of his income into some wise investment may be the smart financial move for an adult with a decent living wage, a man may instead choose to spend his money on perishable things for his enjoyment, using his surplus income to amass toys and collections for himself. To such a man, this is much more satisfying than the ethereal hope of a return on his contribution to a distant and uncertain future. While he may perhaps find a woman that he deems a suitable wife for himself, it is easier to casually date and not commit - or even not date at all - because relationships are so much work and casual sex or masturbation can fulfill his base sexual appetite.

While spending time with his children and offering them guidance especially in the tumultuous teenage years is the right thing to do, it is a challenge. This difficulty causes many a man to abdicate his role as father-leader and instead allow the internet and the other similarly abdicated kids at school to parent and inform their children's moral compass. It's a melting pot of directionless entropy that results in boys who become bigger boys but never men.

In these and many other ways, the Abdicator-led man has tapped out. When the Abdicator is in control, a man is reduced to waking, slumping through the day in a fog, and later going to sleep. He has little to no effect on anything, day in and day out, year in and year out.

This produces a "man of these times" who has no passion and stands for nothing; who is driven by the wind of every opinion around him and every insecurity inside of him. Bly again explains this well: "A man whose king is gone doesn't know if he has the right to decide even how to spend the day. When my king is weak, I ask my wife or children what is the right thing to do."[5]

When a man under-emphasizes the role of King in his life, the Abdicator presents himself, causing the man to be far less than he was created to be. But another imposter lurks nearby who is just as dangerous, and this one emerges in a man when the role of King is over-emphasized.

THE MOGUL

A man whose King is on steroids turns into a Mogul. This tyrant sees leadership not as an opportunity to bring the best for others, but rather to dominate, control, and empower himself.

A Mogul is often very charismatic and winning, and the insecure flock to him because they need leadership. He is able to brainwash and mislead the masses due to his confidence and the impressive results he has seen as a product of his bulldozer mentality. As long as the weak exist to be crushed, the Mogul will build his empire on the skulls of others. Many good people inherently know that this is wrong, but they would rather be on the winning side, and follow blindly. Tragically, sometimes they have no choice.

A Mogul is able to control a room with whatever emotion seems most affecting at the time. A common choice is anger. A boss who shames and intimidates his employees is one example. Consider a husband who controls his wife in the same manner. Very common is the father who assumes the role of Mogul, yelling and screaming at his children in an effort to beat them into submission by the sheer power of his adult-sized temper tantrums. In secret, these children nickname their fathers Napoleon and Mussolini.

At parties or social events the Mogul does the talking, often interrupting others to make sure his knowledge and experience are heard. He often employs a booming voice; he might have memorized a few wordy quotes or be up on the latest football statistics or cultural buzz, stair steps he uses to climb above anyone else who might be prominent in the room. Other times he relies on pure emotion because he has learned from experience that others, in their attempt to converse with him, will give in out of sheer exasperation, yielding to his dominating personality.

Moguls rarely have real friends because they have sent the message to others that they are unapproachable, that it will always be "my way or the highway." Colleagues and even family are reluctant to approach a Mogul about issues with any depth because they know that unless they walk on eggshells, they will touch the exposed nerves of the Mogul and become another subject of his wrath. Instead, they have learned to tip-toe around the problems and accept the fact that the man they are dealing with is an immovable object.

Moguls are emotionally stunted, but because of their willpower, natural charisma or riches they are able to survive without confronting their demons. The relationships in their life tend to have a short lifespan; the Mogul may go through many wives or girlfriends or be constantly looking for a replacement staff person to hire.

For this reason, Moguls are very lonely but stay busy with new exploits in order to keep their mind off of their need for others. When they die, they tend to do so alone. Moguls, after the funeral is over and things return to normal, are remembered not for their good qualities but for those that damaged others, things that were never fair game to discuss while the Mogul was alive. Now, there is finally an end to the dictatorship, a safe place to be oneself apart from the tyrannical reign of the Mogul.

THE DECISION TO LEAD LIKE A KING
Now we come to decision number one; will a man...

- tap out like an Abdicator,
- domineer like a Mogul,
- or, like a King, *courageously lead some great cause in a way that others can follow?*

In making this decision, a man must ask himself a few difficult questions:

- Without thinking too deeply, right in this moment, which of these three do I most identify with?
- If asked, how would the people who are closest to me describe me in this regard?

HOMEWORK
Before moving on, take some time (one day or perhaps one week) to ponder the things you have read about the King and his imposters. Consider these questions as you interact with this material:

1. In the arenas below, are you an Abdicator, a Mogul, or a King?
    a. Work
    b. Marriage, if married; or if not, in a pre-marriage relationship
    c. With my children, if I have any
    d. With my extended family, in-laws, and/or grandchildren
    e. Friendships
    f. Social groups (neighborhood, clubs) and religious groups (church)

2. As you grow in self-awareness, wonder…
   a. Why am I the way I am?
   b. What has positively influenced the King in me?
   c. What has led to the takeover of the Abdicator or Mogul in me?
   d. What past or current life events and memories come to mind as I ask myself these questions?

3. As you think of the future, ponder…
   a. What is my great cause?
   b. What might I remove from my life that would grow the King in me?
   c. What specific behaviors might I start practicing or rekindle to this end?

The Lover

"Love is a pleasing passion, it affords pleasure to the mind where it is; but yet, genuine love is not, nor can be placed, upon any object with that design of pleasure itself." [1] – David Brainerd

Purpose: *To love.*

Decision: *To give oneself to others for their benefit.*

Humans, in our case men, have a tremendous capacity to care for one another. It is said that the four basic human needs are food, water, shelter, and love. The feeling of being loved by another person can change us in an instant. When a man allows the Lover inside of him to be expressed, the people around him feel value and worth. The Lover in man emerges in many different ways – through friendship, through kindness to strangers, through romantic love for a woman.

Whether we spend our life building houses, feeding the poor, performing surgery, or teaching children, the one mark we will have left when we return to dust will be the quality of our impact on others. Jesus tells us that the greatest commandment of them all is to love God, and that the second is to love the people around us, and that everything else hinges on these. Going further, the Bible explains that the extent to which we accomplish the second commandment has a lot to do with whether or not we are really fulfilling the first; it is a litmus test of sorts.[2] If you think you love God, ask the people around you how loving you are – that may be the truest indicator. No doubt the development of the Lover in a man becomes very important.

LOVERS ARE INTERESTED IN MORE THAN BEING NAKED AND HAVING SEX

"Lover" is a word packed with pre-conceived ideas, so it is necessary to distill it down to its more basic meaning. Often the first idea that enters our mind when reading a book about men, once we arrive at the "love" chapter, is that we will discover amazing things that will improve our romantic and sexual life. While this may be true, it has little to do with romance and being naked (at least in the modern sense of what we believe being naked is, which is an altogether different discussion for another time). Those are certainly arenas in which love can function and blossom, but the truth is the very same things that enable a man to love his neighbor or co-worker well are also necessary for him to have a fulfilling relationship with a woman (including the sexual component). Love has a much broader application for a man than mere physical nakedness.

THE LOVER APPROACHES RELATIONSHIPS PRIMARILY TO GIVE, NOT RECEIVE

At the core of any truly loving relationship is the determination of both parties to give more to the other than they take or are given. The Lover working through a husband does not keep score when it comes to who did the dishes or who changed the stinky diaper. In a healthy sexual relationship, the Lover is more focused on the preferences and desires of his wife and less about his own pleasure.

In this regard, the Lover's primary joy is derived from his wife having a satisfying experience, this being even more important than his own physical desires. His satisfaction goes beyond mere ejaculation. It is deeply tied to his partner feeling cared for and her being able to receive his love when she is ready. In this sense, he is physically invited into ecstasy and the experience is mutual - and simultaneous if timed correctly. The wonder of these things cannot be explained in words. Both lovers go to sleep happy and satisfied, feeling a connection that exceeds anything palpable.

The text of the Biblical Song of Solomon is unashamedly erotic – we have a record of a man so nurturing his wife that she passionately invites him into her garden to enjoy its choice fruits.[3] One need not think long to understand what this means. This sort of reciprocated passion makes a mockery out of the whoring that goes on around the world in the name of sex: we humans prostituting ourselves in order to merely find release or feel we are accepted. The reason so many men are unsatisfied no matter how much sex they get is because it is only about them. As long as that is the case, they will forever be starved for something deeper that cannot be fulfilled no matter how many different ways and times they get the thing they call sex.

LOVERS REJOICE WHEN THEIR FRIENDS SUCCEED

In friendships, the very same principles are at work, and the Lover wants the best for those who call him friend. The Lover is alive and well when a man can rejoice in the success of his brother. Once a man was heard saying, "I was very happy with my yearly salary increase until I learned that the one my colleague received was larger." These sorts of competitions and jealousies do not rear their head in the Lover.

He instead sees others being promoted and can rejoice for them as if he himself were promoted. He sees others achieving their dreams, perhaps while he is struggling to realize his own, but is nonetheless happy for them. He buys tickets for a charitable raffle but is satisfied if another's name is drawn as much as he is if he were to win. He loves when somebody succeeds, even if it is not himself.

LOVERS SENSE THE WONDER IN OTHER PEOPLE

The Lover can find transcendence in others. St. Augustine, upon his later-in-life conversion to the Christian faith, writes of the many changes that occurred as a result. Concerning one of them, the entry of the divine into his collegiate relationships, he muses: "I found that I could taste God in friends."[4]

If you can believe it, any good that we experience in people is the glory of the Creator being displayed through them. An epic beard, a beautiful dancer, a rapturous melody – all of these speak of the divine. Something as simple as a winning smile or a quirky mannerism in a person can move the soul. I have seen a woman's exposed shoulder while shopping at the grocery store and felt nothing erotic, only transcendent. The Lover picks up on these things and is drawn not to the creature, but to the Creator. All things are pure to the pure. Seeing these glimpses of glory and beauty in others lifts human interaction to a new level. It also builds equity for future interactions in which we experience the not-so-glorious parts of others.

Many times in my life I have felt as if I began to touch the soul of another human. Sometimes this happens through sharing a deep experience of pain, when one person trusts another with their fragility. Other times this occurs through shared life experiences. Still other times it seems as if the veil between heaven and earth has been temporarily lifted in the midst of a conversation or song or romantic moment. It is in these times that we hesitate even to speak because we do not want to usher the veil back in, but rather enjoy the moment. In these instants, we feel as if we could die with these people. The Lover is alive and well, experiencing the pinnacle of relationship possible between two humans this side of heaven. Or perhaps it is a bit of heaven.

C.S. Lewis has much to say about this type of friendship love: "Eros will have naked bodies; Friendship, naked personalities. [When with friends, a man] sometimes wonders what he is doing among his betters. Friendship is not a reward for our discrimination and good taste in finding one another out. It is the instrument by which God reveals to each the beauties of all the others."[5]

THE LOVER ADDS SOMETHING WHEN HE ENTERS A ROOM

Once I learned a sociological model which contains seven kinds of people. They are +3, +2, +1, 0, -1, -2, and -3. The positive numbers represent those who contribute something in any social setting, while the negative numbers are assigned to people that drain or kill the social vibe. So, a +3 contributes a large amount, a +2 less, while a +1 adds maybe a very small bit; and the same goes for the negatives - you get the picture. The zeros are the wallflowers who neither add nor take anything.

With this in mind, imagine a room of twenty people,

each having a score from the options above. The aggregate of those twenty numbers will determine the overall 'social atmospheric quantity' of the room. This could happen in the context of a neighborhood barbeque, or a church service, or a staff meeting.

The man who is inhabited by the Lover walks into the room and instantly adds. People want to be around him because they feel hopeful. He exudes acceptance; this puts people at ease. He says things that are nice things, not critical or of a peacocking nature. People know they are valuable to him whether or not they dress or act appropriately or know how to speak well. They don't have to be in the "cool club" to be able to approach the Lover. He accepts all people equally without discrimination, even if he disagrees with their religion, politics, or other filters.

LOVERS MAKE OTHERS FEEL GREAT, NOT SMALL

There is an obscure passage in the Old Testament that has transformed the way I look at people. Before rebuking a miserable and suffering Job, his friend Elihu says this: "I am about to open my mouth, but first hear this. I am the same as you in God's sight. Both of us were cut from a piece of clay. Nothing I do should terrify you, nor should my pressure weigh heavily on you."[6]

In this sort of relationship there is no pecking order. One person is preparing to deliver a scathing but needed reprimand to another, but it is done without ego. Instead it comes from a place of humility. That is how the Lover functions in the relationships in his life. Even confrontation is done in a way that does not shrink the hearer.

This type of relationship, without the overlay of power, characterizes the life of the Lover. He is not easy to offend and does not become annoyed by trivial things, so often relational scuffles do not have the opportunity to come to anything. The Lover is able to overlook matters and brush off the chip that might try to form itself on his shoulder.

LOVERS LOVE OTHERS WHETHER OR NOT THEY ARE LOVELY

The Lover shows love to others but it has little to do with their apparent worthiness of this love. A man guided by the Lover can talk to an unattractive woman as easily as he can talk with a beautiful one, and the same is true of the opposite, depending on how one's insecurity manifests itself in this context. He can show up at a party and speak with strangers, perhaps ones very different from himself, rather than finding safety among the usual crowd he might be comfortable with.

This is because his measure of other people's worth has little to do with their loveliness or *his attraction to them*. Neither their abundance of loveliness nor their lack of it becomes a condition of relationship. Love is not given because they are loveable, but because the Lover is loving. Thus, he is free to love, not bound by the possibility of reciprocation or reward that might or might not come in return. He does not see his interactions with others as a way to entertain or increase himself, but rather them.

This is what motivated Mother Teresa to hold diseased and dying people in her arms and clean their wounds. For her it was never about what she was gaining from these encounters, but rather what she was giving. The recipients of her love and care experienced the same freely, without having to earn them or fulfill any qualification.

THE LOVER KEEPS LOVING ONCE THE HONEYMOON IS OVER

A relationship cycle model that is commonly used has four stages: Infatuation, proximity, drama, longsuffering. *Infatuation* is the stage where there can be no wrong, where bliss is the order of the day, and where feeling dictates interactions and is also their reward.

At some point in any relationship – with your spouse, child, job, church, even your car – *proximity* takes its toll. The green grass is suddenly not as green; flaws are noticed now that you are spending time so often with the former object of your infatuation.

Next comes *drama*. Drama occurs because the two people involved, like two porcupines running into one another, are going to draw blood as a result of proximity. Most relationships end here.

If the drama can be weathered, we arrive at *longsuffering*, but it does not have to be only miserable. We choose to continue in relationship even though it may cause us pain. We learn to compromise. Our love matures, and if we are patient enough, we reach a new level of infatuation - and the cycle begins again. The man who is a Lover is willing to wait, to wade through the pain, in order to achieve these deeper and richer levels of relationship.

THE LOVER IS COMFORTABLE WITH ONE-SIDED RELATIONSHIPS

When a man makes a choice to let the Lover do his work he is then able to accept the one-sided nature of many relationships in his life. The truth is, in general, people want to see what they can extract from others for their own benefit. Men use women or images of women for their pleasure, and that behavior drives the most lucrative and long-standing markets on our planet. When I approach the produce stand or buffet, I unconsciously pick the best apples for myself, leaving the rest for future less-important customers. When we meet others, we subtly size them up, planning the future of the relationship in advance, discerning what we might gain from it. This isn't all bad; it's just the way it is.

When the Lover is about, this mentality changes in the context of our interaction with other people. While we keep our nobility and do not let others abuse us, we accept the fact that many (if not most) of the relationships in our lives are going to be one-sided. A great proof of this can be found by simply examining our conversations. Were you to have coffee with another person, chances are that they would be very happy to talk about their life and problems for the entire hour while you listened, or vice-versa.

Again, this is perhaps good and right; sometimes people need a listening ear. But the older we get in life the more we realize that we are only going to have a few friends who will reciprocate this listening. There are few who can relate to us, who have experienced our proximity and our drama and can still belly laugh with us; they are treasures. Most of the other people we associate with are content to take, especially if we have something to give. The Lover in a man realizes this, and for the sake of others he is able to walk into these gardens, sow some new seed, and leave with a handful of weeds but none of the ripe produce.

Another unavoidable aspect of some relationships is that we will cause injury or there will be misunderstandings that cannot seem to be reconciled. For one reason or another (at times we know not why), we realize that we have been written off by someone. They have closed the door to us, perhaps because we have failed them one too many times. This one-sided love is especially important here. In such a relationship the Lover keeps his arms open even if the gesture is not reciprocated.

THE LOVER CARRIES NO BULLETS

A man must choose not to arm himself in the context of such relational drama. I am not saying that you or I should be a willing victim or allow people to mistreat us. However, in order for the relationships in his life to be characterized by depth and grace, a man must choose to empty the chamber in his proverbial gun that represents his grievances against other people.

Yes, some wounds need to be processed; but the truth is that a large amount of conflicts are either not worth solving or not solvable. If a relationship is to be as healthy as it possibly can, we are required to dismiss anything that we could use as a weapon against another. A past misunderstanding might represent one bullet, while a betrayal might represent another, and so on. We must decide to move beyond these for the sake of relationship, choosing not to bring them up again or use them as future ammunition. When we do this, the Lover in us is blossoming, our relationships characterized by deep roots and good fruit.

As a boy I grew up in a home where there was very little love communicated. I have almost no memory of verbal affirmation nor physical affection being given to me beyond about age three. I do remember one time I saw my parents touch, but it was only once, when I was quite young; I remember exactly what my mom was wearing, and what the furniture looked like in the room. This only happened once, and I never saw them hug or kiss. As time went on, they grew further and further apart, and when I was a teenager mom and dad finalized a very bitter divorce.

All of this took a toll on my father, with whom I lived for most of the years that followed until I went out on my own. He went from casual imbiber to full-on alcoholic, and in time his beverage of choice evolved from beer to hard liquor. Then at one point I began finding drugs and needles, sometimes laying on the carpet in plain view. Because of this he lost job after job, and also his license to practice medicine.

All of this combined with other things I will discuss later proved difficult for me; at a certain point I completely despised my dad and I decided to tell him how I felt. It was about the time I became a young man, around age eighteen. We rarely even talked, but one day we were outside walking our family dog, who as I remember was urinating on the neighbor's lawn, and I couldn't take it anymore. I told him that I hated him and that he had never been a father to me.

This only enraged him, leading to some horrible yelling and about a month of no communication. But after a few more months a change occurred. One day dad told me that he was sorry he had not been a father to me, and that he was going to change. That conversation marked the beginning of the final fifteen years of his life and the first fifteen of our relationship as father and son.

In those years that followed I experienced the epitome of bittersweetness. Dad wanted to be in my life, and I kept giving him chances. Trying to have a relationship with an addict over a sustained period of time is extremely difficult, and as time advanced his addiction only worsened. There were a hundred times I wanted to walk out but I never did. I decided that the relationship was worth the price I was paying. I kept going back, offering grace, crowding my way into my dad's life, and met a broken but beautiful person as a result. This experience caused my maturity as a man to grow exponentially. Plenty of bullets kept appearing in my pocket, ready to be chambered, but the gun was never loaded. The Lover was growing in my heart and doing his work.

One windy spring day I was driving through nowhere in Florida, returning from a vacation, and I got a phone call. An insurance agent informed me that my father had just died a horrible death, and later the toxicology report did not hide the reason for the accident. Upon arriving home, I discovered that just a few days before that day my dad had called and left a message on my answering machine while I was away. He said, "Hi guy, sorry I missed you, just wanted to call and say I love you, and I'll see you when you get back from your trip."

While I felt that my soul had been ripped out of my body, there was never one hint of bitterness. The Lover in me had taught me how to keep my chamber empty through the power of grace and forgiveness, and there was simply nothing there to shoot at dad.

Lovers are able to weather difficult relationships without burning bridges. When a man is fulfilling his role as Lover, the people in his life, whether close companions or strangers, experience care. When the Lover is around, they find that they feel more worth and value. Being in the presence of someone that cheers them on can make their troubles seem to have much less weight.

However, if this sort of love is neglected or distorted in a man's heart, one of two imposters will take up residence. When a man undervalues the Lover, he walks the solo road of the Loner; when he indulges in the pleasures of love too much, he transforms into the Hedonist.

THE LONER
The man who neglects the role of the Lover becomes the Loner. Loners have decided that loving others is too hard, or that they themselves are unlovable, and therefore there is no point in trying. Having given up on relationships, the Loner lives a barricaded life with protections in place to make sure nobody gets through.

A man can be a Loner and still have people around. Nevertheless, at some point in the past he became a Loner when he chose to close his heart. He avoids certain types of people. He might have a wife or children he has emotionally abandoned because he has decided that their differences are irreconcilable.

I have talked with many men who are Loners in their marriage. A man in this condition coexists with his former love, sometimes sharing a bed and conversation; but intimacy, romance and lovemaking are all long-gone. He has determined the cost of fighting for these things is too high, so the Loner gives up, possibly in an attempt to manipulate his wife into needing him. This rarely works, especially if the woman is emotionally strong, and the two only grow further apart.

A Loner can sometimes draw a following, but ultimately his leadership is self-focused rather than true servant-leadership. Often the comfort of victimization behavior can sustain the Loner. But he does not really want help because that would necessitate him allowing others to speak truth into his life and for him to become teachable. However, he has a very good act by which he is able to attract others who will enable his narcissism in order to validate their own.

His claims that he is alone, has been ill-treated by so many, that nobody understands him - these all stem from unprocessed character challenges in the Loner's past. Yet when heard by the easily duped, these things actually draw a culture of like-minded people around the Loner. No one will ever really get to know him because he will not remove the humble façade he wears, which is really pride. In these types of relationships love is talked about a lot but the love is never tough love, it is only codependent love. Loners in a group together end up simply stroking one another, licking each other's wounds, but never dealing with any of the causes of the disease.

Not having any true accountability or confession leads Loners to keep dangerous and destructive secrets. Without allowing his unhealthy behavior patterns to be confronted and processed in the context of community, a man will keep a closet full of skeletons. Being alone, whether because he dislikes people or because "nobody understands me," is an effective way to keep these things in the dark. Ultimately all of this will leave the Loner completely alone.

When a man rejects the role of the Lover in his life, the Loner appears, distorting and obscuring one of his most powerful attributes, the ability to care for others. There is, however, another danger: that of over-emphasizing the joys of love in one's life. When this happens, the addictive personality of the Hedonist consumes every potential a man has for love and turns it fully upon himself.

THE HEDONIST

The Hedonist is a leech – a man bent on pure pleasure, expending himself tirelessly to find it.

In healthy love, both giving and receiving take place. As mentioned earlier, we prioritize giving to others, putting their needs before our own, and this makes for a truly loving relationship. In turn, if the friend or spouse is also pursuing these things, we cannot help but experience a flood of reciprocal joy and nourishment from the relationship. This is the receiving part of the arrangement, and it is good when held in balance.

The Hedonist, however, only focuses on the part for himself. He is about and only about what he can take away from another person. A prime example of a Hedonist friend is one who will make plans with you but subsequently cancel them if something else more stimulating comes along. This is proof that he has less interest in you and more in who will bring him the most entertainment at the moment. Loyalty is not his concern.

The Hedonist can especially twist a man when it comes to sex. In this facet of his life a Hedonist-driven man becomes a thrill seeker. It is the thrill of the hunt that drives the man, not the prey itself. Prey is disposable to the Hedonist – his interest is purely in experiencing the excitement involved.

When studying marriage and sexuality in college, I heard a lecture that helped me understand these things. A study was conducted on sexual addiction, and the resulting information pointed to a progression in the addict that was based on thrill seeking. The addict in question, in this case a man, simply began by seeking out a woman with which to have a sexual relationship. This was not enough, so he next experimented with multiple women, then with men. Soon this was not enough to satisfy him, and he next began seeking out the same with underage children. At some point even this was not enough to satisfy his quest for thrill, and he found himself having sex with farm animals.[7]

While this may seem extreme, it illustrates the drive of the Hedonist to achieve thrill and stimulation no matter what consequence it brings upon himself or others. This can also be seen in addictions like gambling, eating, or shopping. A man never has enough when the Hedonist is running things. Just as much or more destructive is when this behavior occurs in the relationships in a man's life. In the wake of the Hedonist's path lies a graveyard of relationships that no longer excite him and have been thrown aside.

Among the many reasons a man may become a Hedonist is this one: He has been starved from genuine love for such a long time that he is now indulging in its extreme. There are times in life that love is scarce for a man, and in these seasons he must be wary of the invitation of the Hedonist. Strong and alluring, it will take over and run rampant in his life.

THE DECISION TO GIVE LIKE A LOVER
Now we come to decision number two; will a man…

- run away from others like a Loner,
- over-indulge like a Hedonist,
- or, like a Lover, *give himself to others for their benefit?*

In making this decision, a man must ask himself a few difficult questions:

- Without thinking too deeply, right in this moment, which of these three do I most identify with?
- If asked, how would the people who are closest to me describe me in this regard?

HOMEWORK
Before moving on, take some time (one day or perhaps one week) to ponder the things you have read about the Lover and his imposters. Consider these questions as you interact with this material:

1. In the arenas below, are you a Loner, a Hedonist, or a Lover?
    a. Work
    b. Marriage, if married; or if not, in a pre-marriage relationship
    c. With my children, if I have any
    d. With my extended family, in-laws, and/or grandchildren
    e. Friendships
    f. Social groups (neighborhood, clubs) and religious groups (church)

2. As you grow in self-awareness, wonder...
    a. Why am I the way I am?
    b. What has positively influenced the Lover in me?
    c. What has led to the takeover of the Loner or Hedonist in me?
    d. What past or current life events and memories come to mind as I ask myself these questions?

3. As you think of the future, ponder...
    a. In what ways do I give myself to others?
    b. What is the most profound benefit I can bring to other people?
    c. What might I remove from my life that would grow the Lover in me?
    d. What specific behaviors might I start practicing or rekindle to this end?

The Fighter

"You can stand me up at the gates of hell but I won't back down." [1]
– Tom Petty

Purpose: *To battle.*

Decision: *To vigorously fight for the right things.*

The very existence of the Fighter archetype tells us that there is an enemy who opposes a man. If he embraces the King inside of him, choosing to stand for something, he will soon be called to fight. Any good cause has a cost, and that is the carnage and chaos of fierce battle. Men choose their side early in life and before long they reach the age when they will inevitably be drafted. This is the time when a man is called to stand up, raise his fists, and enter the fray.

FIGHTERS RUN INTO BATTLE, GRINNING

There is a fire that can rage in a man so fiercely that he welcomes battle. This may burn early or emerge later in life, stoked by circumstance. In either case, a time comes when a man grows tired of fighting his fears and instead begins to fight his fight. This is when his heart has come to the place where the Fighter is summoned, and a man starts swinging.

When he is in proper balance, a man will discern what things he will fight for. Rather than fighting out of his emotion, or for his gain, he fights out of conviction. There are principles he has come to believe are worth his time and money and reputation, maybe even his life. Somehow, when the fire burns, none of that matters, and a man smiles and welcomes the Fighter in him to unleash the fury.

The famous story of David and Goliath is a great example of this. The details of the story are renowned: a teenage Jewish boy, on a mission to ration his soldier-brothers with some cuts of fresh cheese, instead finds himself before a Philistine champion – a man nine feet tall, whose weapons are too heavy for average men to even lift. Without armor or even a sword, David goes to the battlefield alone to fight.

A profound piece of commentary we see within this story is that *David ran to the battle line*. The taunts and verbal abuse from the man everyone else feared only served to stoke this ferocity inside of David. As he entered the battle, his answer to these taunts was one of his own: "I'm going to cut your head off and feed the bodies of all your friends to the birds." He did, and he used Goliath's own sword to do it. The birds ate well.[2]

FIGHTERS INSPIRE THE FIGHT IN OTHERS

Later we learn that the Fighter in David certainly motivated the Fighter in his best warriors, known as his mighty men. Among the crazy commentary on the exploits of these heroes is one passage that describes a group of them as having faces like lions.

"They were brave warriors, ready for battle and able to handle the shield and spear. Their faces were the faces of lions, and they were as swift as gazelles in the mountains. The least was a match for a hundred, and the greatest for a thousand. These were the ones who crossed the Jordan in the first month when it was overflowing all its banks, and they put to flight everyone living in the valleys."[3]

Here again we see the Fighter strong and courageous. Aside from the handling of weapons, there is something symbolic here for us: These men ran into battle, and they did it at a time when the battle was most fierce. The fact that they crossed when the Jordan River was overflowing tells us that they refused to be stopped by even the greatest difficulty. They did not wait until the springtime of life when things come easier. Instead, they took the enemy on his own ground and won anyway. A man possessed by the Fighter will not be stopped. These men knew what David had done and they emulated him.

A FIGHTER POSSESSES COURAGE BOTH ON AND OFF THE BATTLEFIELD

While not many of us will wield such weapons, the Fighter is needed in the wars fought in everyday life. The days of spear and shield are long gone, but in today's times a man still needs the Fighter living sober and strong in his heart.

I have a friend who told me a story that has stuck with me for years. He manages a small business, but one large enough to require a full-size metal dumpster which is parked behind the company building. One rainy day as he was leaving his office he noticed a large work truck around back; several men were illegally dumping construction trash into the dumpster.

Dressed in slacks and a button-up, he approached them and asked them what they were doing. An argument ensued as the men tried to pass the blame on their boss who had apparently told them to find the nearest random dumpster and get rid of their garbage. My friend demanded that they climb in, remove all their trash from out of the dumpster, and haul it elsewhere. The men were not happy but they gave in and got to work. Standing up to a group of foul-mouthed ne'er-do-wells wasn't part of his job description, but the Fighter was alive in this man. My friend ended the story by telling me that he was wearing a pink shirt that day.

SOMETIMES FIGHTERS DON'T TALK ABOUT THEIR FIGHTS

While a Fighter will fight when it is necessary, he is not defined by fighting. He does not find his identity in his ability to win or conquer. Fighting is simply a byproduct of his ethic, and while he will fight, he does not need to fight and probably would rather not fight in many cases.

This type of restraint is rare these days. The modern forms of gladiatorial combat that proliferate in our modern culture have produced a false machismo among men that knows very little of nobility. There are fights, pre-fight discussions and post-fight analysis. The months before a fight of this nature, whether it be boxing or MMA, are a circus of hype designed to stir up the fans and build viewership. The warriors make bold statements about how they will destroy one another, how they are unstoppable, and the like. Talk, talk, talk.

There is a different kind of warrior in the heart of the Fighter. This is beautifully typified in the film *Drive* by a character who is never named throughout the entire movie, simply listed in the credits as "The Driver." This is a lesson in and of itself.

Strong and silent, this man quietly goes about his day fixing his car and trying to stay out of trouble. But when a great cause presents itself – protecting an innocent woman and her son – he exemplifies justice and chivalry in a way rarely seen on the screen, much less the earth, these days. It is then that the Fighter emerges and the antagonists of this story realize they have entered the ring with the wrong person. Before, during, and after the time that the Fighter appears, the driver rarely speaks; in fact, he has very little dialogue in the movie at all. Nobody knew he was a Fighter until it was time for him to fight.[4]

FIGHTERS HAVE SCARS

A Fighter may not talk about his fights, but he is inevitably laced with scars that tell the story without words. The older a man is, the more scars he will have. Scars that are deep enough are visible for a lifetime, and the battles they represent have left a permanent mark on the man who wears them.

A man who has processed his fights in a mature way has grown in wisdom. Sometimes men use their scars to gain attention and bolster their bravado. A wise man lets the scars speak for themselves without explanation or embellishment. Thinking of David's warriors again, men with faces like lions, I imagine men with many scars, like an old, battle-weary lion might have.

Young male lions are handsome, with flowing hair, strapping muscles, and boundless energy. Older lions, however, appear tired. The battles of life have worn them out. Often they have scars on their muzzles, patches of hair missing, perhaps a limp. War has taken its toll. There is, however, a low growl coming from these old lions, and they are still quite capable, if not more capable, of terrible ferocity.

A man that has weathered many battles is like an old lion. His scars should be respected, because they tell a story of a man that has stood up to adversity. The younger man that reverently draws near to an old lion will learn much about the ways of the Fighter.

FIGHTERS GET VICIOUS BUT ONLY SOMETIMES

A wise man has learned lessons from his scars and he knows which battles are the right ones to fight and which should be abandoned. Thus equipped, a Fighter is able to walk away from a fight. He assesses the cost and benefit of each fight before it breaks out and decides if it is the fight for him. The nobility inside a Fighter allows him to do this. He might even walk away from a fight that he knows he can win. Just because you can does not mean that you should. The Fighter aspires to things higher than winning.

The book of Proverbs teaches us again. By seeing through the lens of Jewish thinking we learn much about how a man can, in a sense, exercise control over his temper. One commonly used Hebrew idiom conveys the idea that he does so by deciding to either withhold it or send it out, depending on the circumstance.

In this ancient writing we learn that a man can "restrain his words with a cool spirit," as opposed to one who, rather than holding it back, "sends forth all his spirit," which in our English translation simply reads "loses his temper." Elsewhere, Solomon tells us "Like a city that is broken into and without walls is a man who has no control over his spirit."[5]

The Fighter, when mature in a man, exercises self-control and knows when to release his passion and when to hold it in. The Fighter knows what he stands for and is secure in himself. He does not waste his strength.

SOMETIMES FIGHTERS TAKE THE LONELY ROAD

There are times that a Fighter must fight alone. As is true with the King archetype, the man who embraces the Fighter must learn to leave the company of others and fight some battles solo. Most often the reason for this is not that he has nobody to fight alongside him, but rather that he must in a sense fight with himself in an effort to discover who he is apart from the support of others.

This occurs often in the context of relationships. Even in the seasoned years of his life, a man must sometimes go in a direction that will put him at odds with those closest to him. This includes friends, family, and even his wife. It is not that he cannot agree with others around him, but rather that he must be able to realize his meaning separate from the opinion and approval of anyone else. This is among the most difficult of battles, and it is here that a man may need the Fighter most.

Robert Hicks speaks much to these things in his insightful book *The Masculine Journey*: "We have failed to define our identity, our purpose apart from our relationship with woman…and having sold our souls for her approval, we are ill at ease. To become a man, a son must first become a prodigal, travel solo into a far country…to love a woman a man must first leave woman behind."[6]

When a man does not need the approval of a woman, it is then that he can love her best. It is no secret that wives tend to struggle with being contentious with their husbands. Often in the absence of his leadership a woman will, as a last resort, take the reins in decision making. Other times it is more insidious than that; a wife simply does not want to be under her husband's leadership in any way, for she despises it. This leads to a type of revolt, one in which she picks and prods at him, becoming his constant critic.

It is at this time that the Fighter is essential. Women actually like men who can fight fair. A wife might be butting heads with her man simply because she wants to see him take action. She needs the safety of knowing her husband will do the things that a leader does. She brings her strongest anxiety and opposition, subconsciously hoping he will absorb them and show her a better way. When a man can fight fairly with his woman, standing up for himself while not taking cheap shots at her nor playing the role of victim, things start to happen. When he can stand up to his wife, able to take a blow without sulking or storming off, her respect for him will skyrocket.

A FIGHTER CAN LOSE NOBLY

Another lesson that a man must learn as he embraces the Fighter in his life has to do with losing. Most of us do not make it through our journey without a few losses on our record; sometimes there are many. A mature man has learned that his triumphs and defeats, no matter how many of each he has, do not tell the whole story of who he is.

This again goes back to identity. When we lose, we have a choice: either accept our limits and learn from them, or rage like a two-year old, alternately moping or charging our way (men do both) back to the proverbial gym to beef up for the rematch. Sometimes a rematch is necessary and right, but other times we realize that we have run into a boundary and it is fixed. Rather than achieving something in a victory, we accept that this battle is one where we only learn if we lose. There is no way around this.

This acceptance enlarges, not diminishes, the Fighter in a man, if he can bear it. Then he is free to fail because there is not so much on the line. His ego is no longer tied to his performance in the proverbial ring, so he is not only able to accept defeat, but also able to take more risks because his self-image is no longer so fragile. Those issues have been resolved and he has much less to lose.

Robert Hicks again relates these truths with profound clarity: "When a man no longer feels that he must be a remarkable writer, craftsman, or leader, he is more free to be himself. Chances are he will contribute more to society when his life expresses more of himself."[7] And again, to this point, "...it is no longer essential to succeed, no longer catastrophic to fail."[8]

This marks the full maturity of the Fighter persona in a man. He gives all he has, vigorously fighting for something right, some cause that is worthy of his all. The war has many battles – some he will win, some he will lose – but in the end he will be the victor because the Fighter has nobly led the way.

Robert Bly aptly sums up this achievement:
"When a warrior is in service to a transcendent cause he does well, and his body becomes a hardworking servant, which he requires to endure cold, heat, pain, wounds, scarring, hunger, lack of sleep, hardship of all kinds. The body usually responds well. The person in touch with warrior energy can work long hours, ignore fatigue, do what is necessary, finish the Ph. D., endure obnoxious department heads, live sparsely, write as T.S. Eliot did under a single dangling light bulb for years, clean up shit and filth endlessly like Saint Francis or Mother Teresa, endure contempt, disdain, and exile. A clawed hand takes the comfort-loving baby away, and an adult warrior inhabits the body."[9]

In my younger life I learned much about the Fighter from a karate instructor at a small dojo where I trained for years. The building was a hole in the wall, almost hidden from the public. If a person found it, it was because they were looking for it; there was no advertising, just word of mouth.

Our instructor was a man you have never heard of named Virgil Kimmey, who at the time was about seventy years old. He was a man who had spent most of his life fighting or training others to fight. Calm, humble, but very capable, he knew exactly how to defend himself and hurt other humans. As I advanced in my training under this man, I was gradually invited into the "inner circle" and began to learn more about him.

Mr. Kimmey grew up poor in the Great Depression,

stealing vegetables in order to feed his mother and siblings, as there was no father around. He served in the U.S. Army, and I remember the day he showed me his Purple Heart over lunch at his house. He had trained an Olympic medalist, and he'd won many tournaments himself. He never finished grade school nor earned a GED, but he was awarded a Ph.D. near the end of his life.

At the same lunch meeting (I have no recollection of what we ate, for I had an appetite for other things) he pulled out a large photo album and showed me a picture of himself maybe twenty years younger, standing in the snow, barefoot, in black fatigues, encircled by Green Berets whom he was training in hand-to-hand combat. The further in I got, the more I realized that this man was the real thing.

Despite his high level of badassery, he always told us *not* to fight unless necessary to defend ourselves or someone we loved. He prohibited his students to ever wear their gis (a gi is a canvas karate uniform) in public, encouraging us not to talk about or flaunt what we were learning when we went outside of the dojo. He told us to walk away from fights – not because we were scared, but because it was not right to permanently injure another person if we could help it. It was a privilege to sit under such a humble warrior for many years. Over my time in his tutelage he taught me how to fight, but I learned much more about what a Fighter really is.

When a man trains up the Fighter inside of him, he bravely wars for causes that will benefit other people. He does this in a modest and humble way, while also being capable of terrifying ferocity when the need arises. An inspiration to others, the Fighter stands as an example of what true masculinity looks like, shaming the counterfeits so prevalent in our culture these days.

But as with the other archetypes we have discussed thus far, when a man neglects the Fighter in his soul, one of two replacements are quick to take over. The under-emphasis of the Fighter invites the Coward to mope his way in, while the over-emphasis of the same evolves into a beast known as the Brute.

THE COWARD

A man who refuses to stand up and fight embraces the Coward at the helm of his life. Much like the Abdicator mentioned earlier, this twisted leftover of a man's true potential refuses to pay the price necessary to stand for something. The defining mark of the Coward, however, is that rather than tap out as the Abdicator does, he never even enters the fight. His opponent shows up and there is nobody to fight, so the Coward loses before even trying.

Men become Cowards because they are afraid of confrontation and the possibility of losing sleep or shedding blood in order to overcome obstacles. A man may have suffered much at the hands of others and therefore has decided that it is easier to be a Coward than to tussle with anybody. Still worse are men who seem ready to fight, but when tested, show their true colors. This "all talk" manner is common among Cowards.

This behavior proliferates in today's culture because of the incredible amount of access to virtual social platforms that do not require the user to pay the price for what he speaks. Social media has created an army of keyboard warriors who will argue any topic with raging bluster, saying things to others that they would never say face to face because they would get their teeth kicked in for this type of talk. The Coward hides behind a computer screen, stirring political tension; or behind a phone, living out his fantasies with someone he has never met as the credit card bill rises by the minute.

Whatever the reason a man has allowed the Coward into his life, it ultimately happens because there is no great cause that has riled him up. The Coward is lazy. The embers of his heart, designed for and capable of blazing into a fire, have instead become dormant or completely extinguished. Once his conscience becomes numb and his passion petrified, he is content to simply sit and watch others fight. He might have attained magnificence in an online role-playing game - his avatar a mighty barbarian with unstoppable skill and strength - while in real life he cannot do a single pull-up.

In his very first interview with *Rolling Stone* magazine, Tom Petty, a musician whose career spanned four decades, exhibited the heart of the Fighter, contrasting it with the flabby Cowards all around him in the music business. The write-up celebrated his twangy sound and uncompromising attitude when it came to his music, his brash refusal to settle for anything but the very best he could give to his fans.

Speaking out against the complacent musical establishment of his day, a habit he never gave up, he summed it up well in these statements: "You see all these groups get to the top, get too content and blow it with bad music. Our intention is to stay pissed off."[10]

That is the heart of a Fighter. There is something that agitates him and will not go away. The Coward has lost this drive, and gives up any attitude he once had, accepting a pampered indolence as an easy replacement to his potential destiny.

The Coward would replace the Fighter in us, minimizing our greatness, numbing our vigor, and burying our potential for good. But looming over you and I is another substitute to this archetype. When a man battles blindly without wisdom and reason, he morphs into the warmonger known as the Brute.

THE BRUTE

The Brute is the exhibition of the Fighter at redline, the exact opposite of the Coward. Where the latter will fight for nothing, the Brute will fight for anything. Interestingly, the Brute is also very good at fighting for nothing, which means that sometimes the Brute may really be a Coward in disguise.

But it is when a man rages indiscriminately that the Brute is at the helm of his life. The Brute might have a cause, but it is so over-prioritized in his life that he sees nothing else. I have seen men do very foolish things while the Brute was calling the shots. Once I watched a man in a casino approach a blackjack table, lose five hundred dollars in two minutes, and walk away visibly angry.

The modern popularity of MMA is a glaring example of the Brute at work, a melting pot of Brutes who have finally found a place to destroy others and be cheered on as they do so. As a person who spent years competing in martial arts myself, I completely support the sport of combat as a productive form of exercise and competition. At the same time, I am saddened by the way that violence and bloodlust have replaced art and honor in one generation. There is a fine line between seeing two men compete honorably and watching them try to crush one another. Perhaps the real Brutes in such contests are the people watching from the sidelines, safe from the brutality but all at once being entertained by it.

Beyond such physical contexts, the Brute finds his way into a man's conscience through many other means. The Brute is an expert arguer, often leading men with all the wrong motivations into careers as politicians, lawyers, and preachers. The ability to use one's mental and verbal skill to intimidate others is a sure sign of the Brute at work. A man might carry this into his marriage or other relationships, arguing his case without stopping for one second to consider that of others.

Because of their tendency to shut down other people, Brutes seldom have meaningful relationships. Get enough of them together, however, and you will form a Brute squad. This barbarous mob of unbridled testosterone is well known for lynching, pillaging, rioting, and bullying the innocent. They might look like a band of ancient marauders from the cold north, or a high school football team drunk on their popularity, or perhaps a team of rich executives on Wall Street. In these instances and many more, the Brute does whatever is necessary to get to the top, even if it means standing on the person next to him to get there.

THE DECISION TO BATTLE LIKE A FIGHTER
We have come to decision number three; will a man...

- run like a Coward,
- rage like a Brute,
- or, like a Fighter, *vigorously fight for the right things?*

In making this decision, a man must ask himself a few difficult questions:

- Without thinking too deeply, right in this moment, which of these three do I most identify with?
- If asked, how would the people who are closest to me describe me in this regard?

HOMEWORK
Before moving on, take some time (one day or perhaps one week) to ponder the things you have read about the Fighter and his imposters. Consider these questions as you interact with this material:

1. In the arenas below, are you a Coward, a Brute, or a Fighter?
   a. Work
   b. Marriage, if married; or if not, in a pre-marriage relationship
   c. With my children, if I have any
   d. With my extended family, in-laws, and/or grandchildren
   e. Friendships
   f. Social groups (neighborhood, clubs) and religious groups (church)

2. As you grow in self-awareness, wonder...
    a. Why am I the way I am?
    b. What has positively influenced the Fighter in me?
    c. What has led to the takeover of the Coward or the Brute in me?
    d. What past or current life events and memories come to mind as I ask myself these questions?

3. As you think of the future, ponder...
    a. What things am I vigorously fighting for?
    b. What might I remove from my life that would grow the Fighter in me?
    c. What specific behaviors might I start practicing or rekindle to this end?

The Jester

"A story is told of St. John Berchmans, a Jesuit scholastic who died before he could be ordained. Once, while playing billiards, he was asked what he would do if he were to find out that he would die in a few minutes.

He is said to have replied: 'I would go on playing billiards.'" [1]

Purpose: *To play.*

Decision: *To enjoy life and keep having fun no matter how hard it gets.*

Just the title of this chapter might make one feel that this archetype is less important than the others. Sure, a man must lead, love, and fight... but laugh? Why do I need jesting and fun in my life in the midst of all the struggles I face? How can laughing be just as important as these other more "grown up" archetypes we are studying? I'm a mature man, and you want me to *play*?

The truth is, if I did not think it would confuse the reader and get us off to a rocky start, I might have placed this chapter first. The importance of the Jester cannot be understated. When allowed to be present in a man's life, the Jester will save him from a thousand evils. There are many things in life that will crush a man completely, for he cannot come out from under their weight no matter how hard he tries. It is the Jester that makes these things bearable, and beyond that, opens our eyes to fully enjoy life.

THE JESTER APPEARS EARLY IN LIFE

As we think of the Jester, let us begin by thinking of a general pattern that men tend to follow. A man is born, a little baby; then he grows into a boy, and in these beginning years he experiences some sense of caretaking. This varies greatly depending on one's family situation and socioeconomic status, but suffice to say most babies and little boys receive some level of nurture and happiness. In this early stage of life children are encouraged to play. Whether it be toy blocks in a crib, cartoons on television, or superhero action figures, young boys spend their free time preoccupied with imagination and adventure.

As the adolescent and teenage years come, play begins to wane, replaced with responsibility; this is normal and right. At first it is simple: completing homework, cleaning our room, doing a few household chores. Then it gets serious. I remember the day when, at age fifteen, I began my first real job. Before then I'd done plenty of yard work and that sort of thing, but the day came that I tucked my shirt in, survived an interview, and went to work at a fast-food restaurant. It was terrifying; the real world was now upon me. People were telling me what to do. I no longer had control of my life. I went from playing as many video games as I could to cleaning up other people's urine splattered all over the wall of a public bathroom.

Add to that a few other things - we begin to drive, pay our first bills (if our parents are not still pampering us), and learn to follow the "adult" laws that suddenly have bearing on our lives every day. It's a necessary time of differentiation during which a boy becomes a young man. He gets bigger and stronger and smellier - and hopefully more responsible - and he moves toward adulthood. If he stays on the right trajectory, all of this will erase his illusions of princehood, an existence in which life is only about him enjoying the most fun and pleasure possible. The gritty reality of manhood will set in, and he will grow up.

THE JESTER MUST FIGHT TO SURVIVE THESE YEARS

In this crucible of experience that forms a man, the Jester is easily crowded out, and his absence won't even be noticed at first. Men typically spend their twenties and thirties, and often their forties and later, figuring out who they are. Assuming they do not go the way of the Fool (who will be discussed a bit later), men take off their proverbial pajamas, put their toys in the attic, and take on life as a man should.

This means a job, a career, and grown-up relationships such as marriage and children; each of these forces us to compromise and live differently. I cannot sleep in anymore because I must go to work. There is no longer time to watch all the TV I would like because I must take care of my screaming baby. And, what a shock: I don't get to have sex every day like I thought I would.

I cannot go out with my friends and see the newest hip movie because I must fix my car so I can drive tomorrow. I don't have the money to spend on the hobbies I once enjoyed because I need to pay my mortgage and repair the

HVAC unit. You can likely relate to some of these things.

Aside from all of this, there is an emotional drain that a man faces in these years. His dreams begin to fade as life grinds him down. This is quite normal, and if a man lets it happen he will leave behind some of his youthful idealism, learn his limits, and slowly grow into a sage at which time he will begin to meet his fullest potential. But the process to achieve that end can squash every bit of mirth out of a man's soul if he is not careful. He may have grown into a man, but he has become a crusty one.

Then one day comes retirement. How interesting it is that we begin life playing, kill ourselves working for fifty years, and then spend our last few years (or decades, if we have fortune on our side and have not eaten ourselves to death) trying to play again. Retirees want to play – they play golf, they play travel, they play vacation, they play nostalgia, they play bingo. It comes full circle, but a tragedy all too common is that the Jester is absent in the middle years. Through all of life, not just at the bookends, the Jester needs to be expressed in a man.

THE JESTER PRIORITIZES ENJOYMENT OF LIFE

The wise man will recognize these things before it is too late and he will determine to play. When the Jester is present, a man makes an agreement with his wife, his job, his money, his schedule, and most importantly, his self: *I will find time to enjoy my life*. He realizes that unless he experiences recreation – a word with immense meaning – he will wither away, becoming much less than the man he could be. Recreation is just that – re-creating oneself. When we recreate, we do things that bring about new life in us. We experience a figurative cellular reproduction that refreshes our dreams and renews our vigor. Play begets play. You can be forty-five and still play on the floor with children.

There is a cost to this. The man who plays may seem a

bit odd to others especially if he is surrounded by people that do not value playing. It is also critical that he balances his decision to enjoy life with his responsibility to steward it. The healthy man inhabited by the Jester is sagacious with his laughter and lives appropriately in the tension between amusement and duty.

THE JESTER DOES NOT TAKE HIMSELF TOO SERIOUSLY

At the heart of the Jester is not the desire to have fun, enjoy life, or laugh. These things are all important enough, but something deeper fuels his love of life. He has the ability to disassociate himself from the cause and effect of everything that happens in his life. He becomes increasingly immune to the opinion of others and even his own estimation of his performance. Because he no longer believes he is the center of the universe, he does not take himself too seriously.

Again looking at the wisdom of the Old Testament, we read: "Do not take seriously all the words which are spoken, so that you will not hear your servant cursing you."[2] This is important advice for us to heed. We can be saved from much ruin and vexation by deciding not to give too much weight to what others say or think of us.

When another person brings criticism, among our many possible reactions is to internalize and accept the blow. While this might be productive to some extent, at some point we must resolve that we have made amends, done the best we can with a clear conscience to improve ourselves, and move on. We must choose not to own the guilt and blame that others try to put on us.

We can do this because the Jester is alive in us, not giving matters more weight than they deserve. We admit that yes, we failed, but that does not mean the world is ending, nor that we have to wear a grimace for too long. This mentality can also be applied to everyday life. When it comes to the way you dress, speak, and act, you're not always on trial by everyone else. And even if you were, would it matter?

The Jester thinks not. He can wake up, throw on a wrinkled tee shirt, leave his home without looking in the mirror, engage with the public, and not be too concerned about much of anything. Civility and etiquette are necessary at times, but the Jester also knows how to let his hair down. Oh, the shock! One of us humans does not look like all the others. That man must understand freedom.

THE JESTER UNDERSTANDS THAT THERE IS SOMETHING HOLY ABOUT HAPPY

People of faith tend to be pretty stiff, no matter the religion. If you asked the average churchgoer if Jesus ever laughed, they would probably pause to think about it, possibly citing a few examples where he possibly *could* have flashed a smile. This is sad because the Bible says that Jesus was the happiest human in all of history. Smiling was undoubtedly something he did often; how can a man hold little children and not smile? I imagine that when he laughed it was loud and hearty.

Contrary to what many churchmen think, the God of the Old Testament gives a good bit of permission to his people to be happy; if he endorses such behavior, it must be holy. We are to be happy when we eat, and we can be happy when we work. We are encouraged to be happy when we find a wife, and happy when we have sex. We can be happy about having children, and happy in the pursuits we give ourselves to. Moses says it well: "There, with God very near to you, eat, and be happy in everything you've accomplished as a result of his blessing upon you."[3]

This isn't permission to live in excessive luxury and achieve the highest level of pleasure and ease that we are able. But it is an invitation to happiness as we live our lives, day in and day out. It is a promise of God's presence being with us in all we do, and an encouragement to enjoy life, as doing so is intrinsically acknowledging his presence and blessing. The Jester stops to smell the roses, and he smells God in them. To be happy is to be holy. Perhaps when we become joyful, we are channeling the pleasure that God feels about life. Perhaps he becomes happy when we are happy about something because we are delighting in his goodness in that thing. Maybe being joyful is a taste of what God is like all of the time.

THE JESTER REFUSES TO BE CRUSTED OVER BY ADULTHOOD

As Roald Dahl so wonderfully says, "A little nonsense, now and then, is relished by the wisest men."[4] Nonsense is important, and it might be more so for those tasked with or driven to do great and influential things.

I once watched an interview with Todd McFarlane, an artist-writer who created some of the most famous comic book characters in modern times. This man is world-renowned, his ingenious business savvy only matched by his groundbreaking artistic influence on the modern toy and comic book culture. Aside from being known for those things, he is also a pioneer who fought many battles with the establishment inside which he functioned, broke out of it, and paved his own way for creative freedom.

Commenting on this journey and his struggles along the way, he speaks much from the heart of the Jester alive and well in his life. McFarlane tells of spending time with Steven Spielberg and James Cameron, both famous, top-notch moviemakers with whom he collaborated on one of his projects. He describes them as 12-year-old boys simply having fun, citing the reason for their success: they still have a boyish wonder inside that they've never lost. He then closes the interview with a goofy smile and words spoken by the Jester within: "Today is a good day, I'm not letting adults get to me. There's something to be said about immaturity."[5]

JESTERS ARE HAPPILY OBLIVIOUS, AND THIS PROTECTS THEM

A Jester can sort of float through life without seeming too affected by things that might cause many men to become depressed or come unhinged. The sheer enjoyment of life tends to absorb him to the exclusion of other things, in much the same way a small child would lose himself in this or that. This protects the Jester; the wonder of enjoying one's life can keep a man oblivious to much ill.

C.S. Lewis, speaking from the perspective of a demon named Screwtape who is bent on ruining a certain Christian man, explains this concept well. "The man who truly and disinterestedly enjoys any one thing in the world, for its own sake, and without caring two-pence what other people say about it, is by that very fact forearmed against some of our subtlest modes of attack. I have known a human defended from strong temptations to social ambition by a still stronger taste for tripe and onions."[6]

Once I was seeking counsel from a mentor in my life. My profession at the time made me the object of unavoidable criticism from many people. The weight of it was causing me to doubt myself, and I truly wondered if I was as crazy and awful a person as people were telling me I was. I needed an older man who would talk straight to me, evaluate the accusations from an objective place, and tell me if I was truly in error.

My friend listened, then laughed. He assured me that I was on course and gave me a strategy to deal with these sorts of criticisms: *The goober face.* "Jeff, just listen, maintain eye contact while they dump on you, and when they stop to see how you'll react to their criticism, just give them the goober face." Of course, I wondered what this meant, and it was explained to me.

The goober face is an expression that the Jester has since perfected in me through many opportunities to practice its use. It is simply this: when a person vomits all over you, and it is one of those times that you realize anything you say next will only further incite their offensive, your reply is an expression (maybe coupled with a few words) that sort of says, "Wow! I really appreciate you sharing that with me! I'll keep that in mind, that is really something to think about! Have a great day!" The Jester can disarm the angriest attacker by saying very little, affirming their concerns, and not getting riled up or responding.

Again, Lewis speaks very clearly of this strategy: "Who would not rather live with those ordinary people who get over their tantrums (and ours) un-emphatically, letting a meal, a night's sleep, or a joke mend all?"[7]

THE JESTER IS CRITICALLY IMPORTANT IN OUR MOST DIFFICULT SEASONS

In the midst of one of the harder seasons of my life I had an experience while shopping in one of those decorator outlet stores. I don't even remember what I was looking for, but somehow I ended up in the picture aisle, probably because I enjoy looking at art. Maybe I was unconsciously searching for some comfort as I was in a season where I felt I was failing in every single area of my life, particularly my marriage. I could not connect with my wife; after a prolonged period of trial, we had spent all of our relational equity and were deep in deficit. We loved each other dearly, but the sustained pressures of life had brought us to a place where the fire between was reduced to embers, barely smoldering at all.

Among a hundred others, one piece of art froze me in my tracks. The painting is called *The Singing Butler* [8] by Jack Vettriano; perhaps you have seen it too. I do not know what Jack intended when he painted this, but I was instantly and deeply moved.

Under an ominous sky, an impeccably dressed couple dances on the beach. The woman is wearing a red dress and is barefoot. An obviously frustrated servant and a maid hover nearby with umbrellas, but the couple has left the protection of these; they are oblivious, whimsical and carefree. The storm does not matter, the rain does not matter, the thunder does not matter. Their finest clothes can get dirty, their hair can get sopping wet. They do not care; all that matters is the dance.

I stared for way too long at this painting. As simple as it seems, this moment was an epiphany to me and in those few seconds I received strength to keep going. I saw myself and my beautiful wife in this couple. There was no reason to dance, not one. But somehow we were still in, still going, still fighting for hope. We could survive, even *thrive*, in the midst of unthinkable difficulty - and we did. The Jester grew in my life significantly in that season, keeping me going, even laughing, through it all. The dance of our marriage continued, and in due time the clouds cleared and the sun shone down again.

After giving birth to three boys and two fetuses, my wife brought our little girl into the world. I remember the day well. We were pretty scared because it was a high-risk pregnancy fraught with difficulty. At one point we considered flying a thousand miles northward to a cutting-edge hospital where the doctors would perform surgery on our daughter while still in the womb. Thankfully, that did not happen.

Still, because of the complications, there were fifteen medical personnel in the delivery room when the moment came. When Abbey was born, I was sure she was dead because she was purple and was not moving; her Apgar score was a solid two out of ten. I remember that my wife immediately asked me if our baby was okay, and I stalled because I had no answer for her. But eventually things seemed to work out, and after some time in the NICU we took our daughter home.

The next years were difficult. Numbers help tell the story – twelve surgeries, five thousand therapy appointments, two aneurysms, and nine years of life on a feeding machine, to briefly summarize. One day early on she stopped speaking and making eye contact completely, which was a blow. The world of special needs and severe disability became the norm for our life. We were put in the "medically complex" category since we were dealing with four different diagnoses at once. When I stop to think that we have put twenty thousand miles on our minivan making trips to the hospitals and clinics, I wonder how my wife and I have kept our sanity. There has also been financial strain and a measure of loneliness in this experience. When I hear random kids at the elementary school make jokes about "the retarded girl" as my daughter and I walk by, I am not sure how I should feel.

I will fast-forward through the bulk of our experience. People going through these things can find a new normal for their life and make adjustments. They go through stages of shock and grief and acceptance and hopefully resolve as the years mount up. These days we have seen tons of progress; my little girl functions in society in a way that is very different from typical kids, but I kind of love it.

Once when she was still small (she is very small), around nine years old, I dared to take her to the barber shop with me. The probability of public humiliation is always high for us, but I had her in tow and I needed a haircut badly, so I decided to risk it. The truth is, in our world, you just have to live your life and not care if people look at you all the time. I could tell a hundred such stories, but this is one.

As my hair was being trimmed, my daughter sat in the nearest empty chair, talking to everyone. She is incredibly smart, so after a few minutes she pretty much had control of the room, asking everyone around all sorts of random questions about their lives – their names, what kind of car they drive, and the like. Suddenly, the familiar song *Free Fallin'* played on the radio overhead. Her eyes opened all the way, a huge grin hijacked her face, and she yelled out "I LOVE TOM PETTY!" And for the rest of my haircut she sang along at the top of her lungs, to the amazement of all the patrons. Everyone was smiling. How does she know all the words to this song? How does she know who Tom Petty is? Why does she show no restraint?

We got out of there alive and I'm sure we were the talk of the room once we did. Fortunately, this was one of her more civil and cuter moments; it could have gone much worse, as autism is not very predictable by any means. But we smiled the whole way home and sang more Tom Petty pretty loud together as we rolled down the road. The Jester was on autopilot in her unpretentious, impossible-to-fake-it brain.

I was getting there too. Who cares what people think? We're doing the best we can and it's broken but it's great. I can laugh at the mess and I can laugh in the mess. It's in these times that the Jester saves our souls and keeps us going.

When a man embraces the Jester, he is able to celebrate the joys and struggles of life with a smile. He doesn't take himself or others too seriously and has learned to laugh even in the midst of trial. This laughter is good medicine, and it will save a man from a boring life and an early death.

But it is very easy to send the Jester packing at an early age, and when a man does so he is in grave danger of having his manhood held hostage. He who neglects the Jester is taken over by the Prude, while the man who indulges too much in the frolicking nature of the Jester becomes the Fool.

THE PRUDE

When a man stops smiling, the Prude is close at hand. This fiend inhabits a man when, because of wounding or pride, he unconsciously begins looking for coping and defense mechanisms. The Prude is sly and tricky, presenting himself as an alternative to the Jester. When a man cannot enjoy his life as he desires, he opts for the Prude in an effort to barricade himself from the costs that accompany joy in life and relationships.

Just as the name suggests, the Prude is smug and emotionless. A Prude will appear to be above jokes and whimsy, having no time to waste on such nonsense. In his mind, the Prude has advanced to a level in his relationships that requires no silliness. He has become immune to fun and would rather do his own thing. Occasionally this man might take a quick glance back at the Jester life, but his Prude pride quickly reminds him that he is above that, so he steels his gaze and quickly wipes away the subtle grin that had begun forming on his face.

The most common thing that invites the Prude into a man's life is the longstanding grudge that he is holding against a person or group of people. Catastrophe is imminent if a man feels this way toward his wife. Men differ as to how long they can hold such grudges before they desiccate and become a Prude; in some men it happens instantly, in others it can take a few years, but not often more. At the heart of it, the Prude becomes a useful front behind which a man can hide his feelings.

If he is able to keep a straight face, not entering into the joy of things, he can deflect any relational need. Were he to laugh, "get the joke," and let his guard down, it would show that his grudges against others are losing their impact, that he is softening. The Prude keeps a man safe from needing anything from anyone, and with smug disregard he is able to maintain his falsely stoic appearance. Were he to understand what the word *stoic* means, he would behave differently; but because the Jester has left, his heart is distorted as is his understanding of these things.

Another reason the Prude takes over is pride. This is different from the pride that was just described, which involves a man rejecting his need for others – he closes his heart and hands and will not receive help or assistance. That pride is a subtle form of passive-aggressive manipulation.

This other pride is more straightforward. In this case, the Prude simply believes that he really is above others. He believes that they are on more of an animal level since they indulge in things as elementary as they do. He is the classic "fuddy dud" – a killjoy that enters the room and immediately extinguishes all the fun. People know that his presence serves as an immediate judge to their actions, which he deems to be a waste of time.

This sort of Prude shuts down many innocent parties among his children. He is the man who yells at them for getting dirty when they go outside - as if there was no dirt out there that might find its way onto them, being that they were outside and all. The Prude cannot be happy when others succeed, nor will he rejoice with them. He might stop in for a birthday celebration or a good-bye party, but only for a moment, out of obligation – he has more important things to attend to.

When it comes to money, the Prude is a tightwad. Prudes tend to have money, but often see pleasure-directed expenditures as a waste. This applies only to others, however; a Prude will spend large amounts of money on himself but think nothing of it.

The Prude is quite dangerous and can cause a man to grow gray hair far too early and begin to mummify even while he still maintains a pulse. But as the diminishment of the Jester can cause the heart of a man to distort, so can the opposite. A Jester acting without reserve causes a man to mutate into the dimwitted caricature known as the Fool.

THE FOOL

Decadence and debauchery characterize a man when the Fool runs rampant in his life. Just the mention of his name evokes sneers and snickering; his antics and tomfoolery are well-known to all, for everybody talks about him. They might never say it to his face, or they might; in either case, it is clear to any audience watching him that he is a Fool. Some men are even paid to be Fools.

A man who is a Fool is, at his core, seeking attention. The trouble for him is that he has taken this need to the extreme. This desire to be noticed causes the Fool to actually find his identity in being the laughingstock and brunt of jokes. A man of this nature does wild and crazy things to impress others, often to his own hurt. He takes jokes too far, abusing sensibilities without discretion.

Fools tend to go to the extreme in many areas of their lives, often citing their "addictive personalities," though this declaration is actually nothing more than a clever-sounding disclaimer for their lack of self-control. The Fool is known to be the first one who gets drunk at parties. He tends to order dessert even though he had a soda pop with his meal. Again, the key flaw in the Fool is that he over-indulges in the joys of the Jester, making pleasure a norm that he craves regularly rather than a treat that he enjoys on occasion.

This lack of self-control brings abasement to the life of the Fool; nobility and self-respect have left him a long time ago. A sad reality is that the people in a Fool's life have come to accept that this is how he is which often causes them to pity, detest, or avoid him. Men like this tend to drive like idiots and fart indiscriminately in front of their wives.

Another characteristic of the Fool is that he has not

grown up and taken on the challenges of adult life. Addicted to pleasure and fun, such a man might be far into adulthood and still live with a parent. A Fool continues to live in a fantasy world in which he is the prince; his life, from wake time until sleep time, is primarily ordered around him having fun. In many cases, men like this have spawned children somewhere in the world but do little to be present in their lives.

Were a Fool to be honest with himself, he would acknowledge some deep pain in the recesses of his soul. Rather than medicating his heartache with fun and pleasure, he would address the true disease in his heart that lies behind his inability to grow up. Often this involves some self-awareness where one addresses issues of emotional brokenness and begins to actually deal with his destructive ways of thinking and find healing. This, however, would require a major paradigm shift for such a man. For this reason, the Fool remains on top, suppressing the ache and allowing the symptomatic immaturity that serves as a numbing agent to be the negotiator in his life.

THE DECISION TO LAUGH LIKE A JESTER
We have come to decision number four; will a man...

- snub like a Prude,
- revel like a Fool,
- or, like a Jester, *enjoy life and keep having fun no matter how hard it gets?*

In making this decision, a man must ask himself a few difficult questions:

- Without thinking too deeply, right in this moment, which of these three do I most identify with?
- If asked, how would the people who are closest to me describe me in this regard?

HOMEWORK
Before moving on, take some time (one day or perhaps one week) to ponder the things you have read about the Jester and his imposters. Consider these questions as you interact with this material:

1. In the arenas below, are you a Prude, a Fool, or a Jester?
   a. Work
   b. Marriage, if married; or if not, in a pre-marriage relationship
   c. With my children, if I have any
   d. With my extended family, in-laws, and/or grandchildren
   e. Friendships
   f. Social groups (neighborhood, clubs) and religious groups (church)

2. As you grow in self-awareness, wonder...
   a. Why am I the way I am?
   b. What has positively influenced the Jester in me?
   c. What has led to the takeover of the Prude or the Fool in me?
   d. What past or current life events and memories come to mind as I ask myself these questions?

3. As you think of the future, ponder...
   a. What do I enjoy about my life?
   b. How do I spend time and money on recreation?
   c. What might I remove from my life that would grow the Jester in me?
   d. What specific behaviors might I start practicing or rekindle to this end?

The Artist

*"Tabby the cat loved Mr. Putter's tulips. She was old, and beautiful
things meant more to her."* [1] – Cynthia Rylant

Purpose: *To create.*

Decision: *To make and enjoy beauty that is transcendent.*

The Artist in a man represents a seed in his soul that is
bursting with creative expression. Whether or not a man is
interested in the humanities, the Artist is within him,
waiting to bloom in some way. He might draw, paint, sing,
or dance; or he might not. The Artist is not limited to these
sorts of things. When a man embraces this archetype, he
expresses beauty by creating something, and that something
shines of something else even greater. Song, sculpture, and

rhyme flow from his heart; or, if he is of a different flavor, he might produce a beautiful garden, a unique car, custom woodwork, or an intricate architectural blueprint.

He is not limited to only creating art; the regular enjoyment of it, regardless of its origin, is equally important. The Artist is inspired by the beauty all around him. The taste of a mushroom sautéed in butter and fresh herbs evokes something, and it is the Artist who recognizes it. A man can look at the beauty of a woman and, without being stimulated sexually in any way, appreciate it for its own sake. That is the Artist alive and well – smelling, seeing and experiencing life around him as something that ascends to and speaks of another plane of reality.

THE WORK OF THE ARTIST AROUND US IS INESCAPABLE

Creativity is the purpose for which the Artist exists. We grow up unconsciously assuming that all the amazing things around us every day have simply always been there, but that is not true. Much of what is all around us making our lives work - and work beautifully - is there because of the spirit of the Artist.

Think of it. Once long ago a man imagined up a thing called an automobile; none existed before it. An Artist tinkered incessantly until he created a light bulb, by which you now see once the sun sets. All over the earth there are incredible buildings designed by Artists. In the ancient world structures still stand, rising to the sky on foundation stones each as big as a dozen elephants. The engineering behind such feats is bewildering.

It was Artists who reconstructed the skeletons of dinosaurs to give us a glimpse of these amazing creatures. The same are responsible for the printing press, the miracles of modern medicine, the microchip, and the space shuttle. Design, creativity, imagination, inventiveness – our world is better because of the Artist.

Beside all of these marvels is the conventional art that we recognize all around us. Whether it be a beautiful painting, sculpture, song, or dance, the spirit of the Artist creates these and more; because of them we enjoy our life more and are able to transcend the tangible world. This is the reason people fill stadiums to watch and listen to such spectacle – it is a truly transcendent experience, one pregnant with divinity. The wind blowing behind any art is meant to give us a whiff of something beyond. Art takes us somewhere, and the Artist is the one who initiated the expedition.

THE ARTIST BRINGS FRESHNESS AND COLOR INTO LIFE

As we study the different archetypes presented in this text, there might be a temptation to put a low emphasis on the Artist. When you thumbed through this book before sitting down to read it, I wonder if the mention of the Artist threw you slightly off guard. Like the Jester, the Artist is one that may not be the first thing we think of when considering important qualities of manhood. *Men need to work and conquer; Artists never get anything done*, one might think. But I maintain that the Artist has a vital role to play, giving life to a man and those around him through the creative spirit flowing out of him.

Think for a minute before you write off the Artist in yourself or others. Imagine a world where every building, every piece of clothing, every meal you ate was the same. Envision never hearing music, a world without song. Think of how inspired you feel watching a dance routine and consider if dance did not exist. Imagine all the times you have been transported by art and beauty, and then imagine that these experiences never happened. A world without the influence of the Artist would be a dull and lifeless place. But the world is smattered with creativity; the signs of it are inescapable, flagrantly displayed before us every day.

Whether the beauty of a bird in flight or the taste of fresh strawberries, the enjoyment we experience in anything finds its origin in the spirit of the Artist.

THE ARTIST'S ROOTS TRACE BACK TO THE BEGINNING OF TIME

The opening sentence of the most published book on the planet tells us that in the beginning – that is, the start of things as it concerns we humans – God *created*. The very first thing that God did, at least as it affects our history, was that he *made art*. The essence of the Artist reaches all the way back to this event.[2]

If this was the first act of God, then we reason that before he did anything else – lead, love, fight – he created. Interestingly, when man was created, his job description was simple: tend to the creation; cultivate and caretake the garden; give names to the interesting things that were hopping, fluttering, and dashing all around him. Going further, we are told that *we* are made in the image of God. When something is made in the image of something else, it retains some qualities of the original. In this case, we humans pulse with artistic energy because it was by that energy we came to be. We create because we were created.

Therefore, the creative acts of the Artist smell divine. Sure, they can be corrupted and lose that fragrance; but the ability to draw, write, make melody, and invent are all telltale signs that we are being *like* someone else. The transcendent power that leaks out of art does so because of that correspondence. In the Celtic understanding of spirituality there is the idea that there are "thin places" in life. These are opportunities in which the membrane, as it were, between the heavenly and earthly realm is frightfully and wonderfully thin. The Artist can transport us into these places and beyond.

ARTISTS UNDO THE EVIL AND CURSE UPON THE WORLD

If a man cannot believe there is something divine in the world, even in the midst of all its many evils, he would assign the beauty of a ballet to an equal level with the process of garbage disposal. If there is no absolute good, then all is relative and the sense of beauty and justice that we might feel has no beginning, end, meaning, or consequence.

But if a man does believe in good then he must also by logical conclusion believe in evil, for by definition each necessitates the other's existence. And if that is true, then this evil we are speaking of has a plan - a very bad plan - it wishes to unleash upon mankind. As much as the Artist can lift, inspire, and heal through his power, the contrast exists to crush, demoralize, and kill.

In this sense, by the very act of creating the Artist is on the offense. Back to the Old Testament – we were made in the image of God. Ever since then, there has been a great battle going on for your soul and my soul and the soul of every human that will ever be. That battle is very simply this – God wishes to restore us to his image, an image of beauty, rightness, justice, and kindness; again, the image in which we were originally created. In contrast, the Devil wishes to remake us, to re-create us (who were once made to be beautiful; humans are the ultimate art) into his image, which is the opposite of all of that: harshness, evil, oppression, and cruelty.

God creates things; their destiny is eternity. The Devil destroys things; their destiny is entropy. Art can be used to mold people into either image. A man, through the Artist living inside of him, can influence others and bring hope and peace and life. The power of the Artist to do this should not be underestimated.

THE ARTIST ENJOYS THE JOURNEY MORE THAN THE DESTINATION

With all of this as a background, let us now consider the outworking of the Artist in a man's life. While a man might make art for a living or with a view to influence others, he creates art first for himself. To do any differently is to prostitute the creative gift and deny the very reason for which it exists. We create to create, not to make millions or draw followers. Any creative who abandons the means for these ends will give away part of his soul.

It is the journey of the Artist that motivates him. The finished product is all good and well, but the creative process is where the magic happens. Oftentimes we lose the best and deepest impact of art because we are so ready to assimilate it, package it, then peddle and sell it to anyone who is buying.

Think for a moment of the last movie you watched. Unless they were waiting for a bonus scene at the end, chances are that the majority of the audience stood up and left the theater once the credits started rolling. Even if we do stay till the end of the credits, how often do we actually read them? That is the time useful for checking text messages that were missed during the movie. We are so used to gorging ourselves on the two hours of film in question without even beginning to think of the art involved – the stunt people, the special effects team, the workers who built the sets, etc. In the lust for entertainment, we often lose art.

Another example of this: Consider the last album that you listened to. Do you know who played drums or who sang backup vocals? Who actually wrote the songs? How were they recorded? Back in the old days people spent time writing liner notes and then other people spent time reading them. When purchasing the part of the art that you listen to (the music), you also got a bonus - the part you read. In these liner notes one could discover all sorts of interesting things, not to mention cover art and pictures. Nowadays, music and art are more disposable than ever, listened to once or twice as background music and then lost in a sea of cheap entertainment.

THE ARTIST VALUES DEPTH OVER QUANTITY

Tom Scholz, the creative genius behind the band *Boston*, teaches us much about the Artist. After becoming famous and leaving his mark with his first two albums, he slowed down and took a different approach for his third album, aptly titled *Third Stage*. Printed in the liner notes are many interesting things, one of which is pair of blaring sentences reading "No synthesizers used. No computers used." An electrical engineer as well as a rock star, Scholz actually created his own effects for the album. He worked countless hours in his basement soldering circuits to create the sounds heard on the album. A distorted guitar, a bell, even a rocket blasting off - all of these were made the old-fashioned way.[3]

This is a great illustration of the Artist alive and well in a man. The creative process is not subverted with the touch of a button. It is not cheapened, and it means something.

To illustrate differently, consider the food you have eaten today. There is a broad range of flavor and quality of food available to us these days. Hormone-fed beef or chicken that is grown quickly in order to make the most amount of money, and then served at a fast-food restaurant, tastes and is enjoyed very differently than natural foods that are prepared by actual chefs and treated as edible art.

I remember the first time I grew broccoli in my backyard. Up to that time, I had eaten broccoli for decades, and I was sure that I knew how broccoli looked, smelled and tasted. The stuff that came out of my dirt, however, was very different. A deep-bed garden, full of rich soil and mulch but without pesticides, produced something I had never seen before. The heads of broccoli were twice the size of what I could buy in the stores and they looked very different. Sure, we lost a few to grubs, but that did not matter. Even the green color was so much deeper and richer than what I had previously thought was the color of this vegetable. Biting into it, feeling the juices and texture in my mouth, was a surprise, as was the taste. I felt as if I was eating a whole new vegetable that needed a new name - something perhaps from Eden's garden.

Another poignant example of depth over quantity is the camera frenzy in which we find ourselves these days. A picture is worth a thousand words, but a thousand pictures might be worth nothing. The availability of cameras in our pockets has created a culture of people who are increasingly numb to art. We might get more from life if we were to stop photographing the cute puppy moment and just enjoy the puppy itself. Pictures of a sunrise never quite capture the way it looked in real life. How about putting the camera down and just enjoying the moment? The Artist is the one among one hundred who is doing that.

People are so rushed to take a picture of this or that, to catch it on video, to post it on social media, that they don't even enjoy the event itself. I have watched a frenzied mother capturing her daughter's gymnastics performance on a too-large cell phone thing, a wince on her face the whole time. She barely even looked at her real, live daughter – rather she witnessed the event on a screen a few inches from her nose, then rushed to upload it here or there. This documentation will be watched a few times, and then forgotten, maybe stored on a hard drive somewhere. While Facebook was receiving a clip of the routine, the mother thumbing away with expert speed, her daughter was looking out to see if mommy was noticing any of her performance.

ARTISTS STOP AND SMELL THE ROSES
These are all examples of why it is so healthy for a man to embrace the Artist within. When he does, he will enjoy life

for what it is. He will express creativity and notice the beauty all around him, interact with it, and allow it to influence him. Ultimately, this will draw him into heavenly things and produce a depth of character that is rare among men these days. As said before, the Artist is an essential personality that brings color and wonder to our souls.

There is a scene in the film version of *The Secret Life of Walter Mitty* that illustrates this well. Sean Penn plays Sean O'Connell, a world-famous photographer. He is perched on a snowy crag in the middle of nowhere in search of an elusive feline known as the "ghost cat," camera ready. Ben Stiller plays Mitty, a man whose journey has at that moment led him to a conversation with the enigmatic cameraman. As they are discussing life, enveloped in a wintry white landscape all around, the snow leopard suddenly appears. Both are shocked, but the look on O'Connell's face is one of slow and stuttered wonder. Mitty anxiously questions him, perplexed as to why he is not taking any pictures to document this ultra-rare moment. The reply: "Beautiful things don't ask for attention. If I like a moment, I don't want to have the distraction of the camera. I just want to stay…in it…right here."[4]

Here again we see the Artist. A man inhabited by the Artist takes in beauty and lets it change him. And, as a result, he changes others. Some of the best art in the world resulted from an encounter that the artist had with something transcendent. Whether gazing on a sky full of stars or a rare snow leopard, the Artist lets the sacred have its way with him, and he is better for it.

THE ARTIST WILL CREATE OR DIE TRYING
Morgan James is one of my favorite singers of modern times. Not only can she sing the phone book, but when she sings there is something else happening. The tone of her voice, the look on her face - there is an unction present that is hard to find in music these days. When you listen to her it

becomes immediately clear that she sings because she *must* sing. And when she does, she means every syllable of every word.

Here, the Artist is alive and well. Listening to her talk about art is just as moving as hearing her make it. In a promotional piece for one of her albums she discusses what jazz singers call "the riff." Riffing happens when a musician or singer goes outside of the musical blueprint as it were; their emotion, their soul leaks out through the guitar or saxophone or vocal inflection, and something special happens. Watching a blues guitarist riff on a worn Fender Telecaster is an experience. You can tell that something too deep for words is happening inside; the guitar is merely translating.

Discussing this phenomenon, James says this: "The best soul singing goes back to a wail…there can be happy blues, but it all goes back to a longing, a desperation, a wailing, a crying out…everything that we now know as riffing was just some variation on wailing…bigger, louder, longer. It's not for nothing, and it's not for play."[5]

This is the essence of the Artist. When a man embraces this archetype, he is characterized by depth and beauty. He makes things for the sheer pleasure of making them. In doing so, the fire inside of him is stoked and blazes bright, warming everyone who comes near, drawing them into wonder, inspiring hope and goodness.

Ever since I was a little boy I have loved to draw. I would draw anything – super heroes, dragons, the kid in the desk in front of me; whatever caught my eye. It wasn't until age 19 that I delved into music, at which time I borrowed a cheap guitar and learned a few chords.

Then I learned to sing a bit, and before long I was

doing so in front of others. This was a good experience, but something in me still felt unfulfilled. I realized that I wanted to say something myself through music rather than only saying and singing what others had written. This itch led to me scrawling ideas down on random scraps of paper, and before long, these scribblings became a song.

One song led to two, which led to twenty, which led to several hundred. As the years rolled on, I invested thousands of hours in this creative process and learned more and more about the craft of songwriting. In time, I began to arrange and produce and was able to create several albums of original tunes. My songs spread around a bit, other people started playing them, and a few of them were picked up and published by a grassroots record company. A small bit of notoriety and income came as a result, and while having my music published was never my goal, I must admit it is a great feeling to hear stories of my songs being heard on the local radio or played across the world, or have strangers walk up to me on occasion and thank me for a song that inspired them.

Rewind a bit though. Of the five hundred or so songs I've composed, there are a few that have made it to a wider audience and another few that are more personal songs just for me. Not long ago, in conjunction with the release of an album that featured my best writing and production yet, something interesting happened. I got a random e-mail from a stranger asking for the tabs for one of my songs. It had been over a decade since I'd written that particular tune, and I'd sort of lost track of it. A friend had posted the song online, and this person heard it and somehow (I still do not know) obtained my e-mail address and contacted me. They wanted to sing the song at some event and needed the tabs. I was quite surprised by this, especially since the version that was streaming was just a guitar and a few vocals recorded by a junk microphone in a storage room.

The deeper reason for my astonishment was this – that song was one of my secret favorites. It kind of went nowhere, or at least until this moment I hadn't heard much feedback on it at all, but it was dear to me. I wrote it all alone long ago on my birthday. I remember it very clearly: it was a fall day in November on which I packed some granola bars and my guitar and wandered out into the woods. I sat there among the beauty of the forest and wrote the full song start to finish in about an hour. Usually it doesn't happen that way, but this was the exception. Pure inspiration. Only a few people heard it at the time, but those who did loved it.

All those years later, the song resurfaced as if from the grave. As I was releasing a new album of very well-produced and well-funded music, this e-mail served as a contrast of sorts. While I absolutely love the newer stuff, when I compare its high production to the low-res hippie experience in the woods, I have to say that it was under the trees that the more magical moment happened. That song never really made any waves in comparison to my newer stuff, but it lives in my heart as a more sacred piece of art.

Through these experiences, I have come to appreciate the Artist maturing in my life. Whether crafting songs, writing this book, building a shed, or baking homemade pumpkin bread, I feel the pulse of something greater than myself resonating in and out of me. The Artist glows most when a transcendent moment happens, and one of the brightest of such rendezvous for me was all alone under an old oak tree singing to nobody.

The Artist, when active in a man's life, leads to creative expression and enjoyment. Whatever form this art takes, it generates a beauty that is transcendent. This mystic quality rises above the things of earth and brings life to both the man who created it and everyone in proximity to its aroma.

But standing ready to hijack the good work of the Artist are two phonies that would take his place. The undervaluing of the Artist allows the Copycat to sidle into a man's life, while the overvalue of the same gives way to the nonsensical fantasies of the Dreamer.

THE COPYCAT

When every bit of imagination and originality has been sucked out of a man's soul, be sure that the Copycat is present. This chameleon robs a man of the qualities that make him special, replacing them with a milquetoast personality. Blend in, follow the trend, play the game – these are the motives of the Copycat.

Men embrace the Copycat out of insecurity. Rather than being comfortable in their own skin, they look around them and find what is popular, and emulate it. This protects them from being noticed for who they might really be, and rather allows them to appear as what is acceptable to the masses who are also controlled by the Copycat. They often travel in large mobs, using one another as mirrors by which they coddle their delicate egos.

This reality applies to a man's appearance, choice of words, and pretty much every other hint of personality that might exist in his soul. The Artist values being naked, in the sense of being real and unpretentious; there is little to no divide between who he really is and who he presents himself to be. In contrast, the Copycat knows little of such innocence and is an expert at covering himself with every changing trend and style. Masses of Copycats rush to the store, buy the same hats and shoes and hairstyles, and join the herd, secure in their insecurity.

I recall once in elementary school when I was rather smitten with a particular fourth grader. This crush had been years in the making, but in all that time the girl barely knew my name. The thing to wear in those days was a popular jacket branded "Members Only." How ironic this name is in retrospect. All the cool kids had one, and it seemed like I was one of the only boys who did not.

Somehow, near the end of that school year, my mom bought me a jacket. I remember it very clearly — it was burgundy, a rare color, but nonetheless it was a jacket. Upon closer inspection I was quite disappointed to find out that it was not an *actual* jacket; rather it was a knock-off bought at a clothing store where losers shopped. No matter, it certainly looked like the real thing. The same day it was given to me I removed the tag, donned my super suit, and took my red Huffy bike for a ride through the neighborhood.

I remember exactly where I was, on what street, in front of which house; it was on a slight incline. As I pedaled uphill, who should be riding down the hill toward me but the love of my life. It was like a commercial — her hair blowing in the wind, her pink bike rolling along in slow motion, her face a fantasy. As she approached, my heart beat faster and faster, and to my surprise she spoke once she was near enough. She offered only one sentence as she passed by: "Jeff! I didn't know you had a jacket!"

The exhilaration lasted about half of one second. Then, rather than feeling the pluck and pride I had so desired, I felt a deep shame. I was embarrassed. Not because the jacket was a fake — she wasn't close enough to notice that. The indignity I felt so strongly came from a realization that I had sold out. As soon as I was like her and all the others, and it was pointed out, I saw myself as I was: a follower, a spineless grub vying for position in a sea of maggots, a brainless clone, a fake of the worst sort. I felt like I died in that moment.

I turned around, went home, took the jacket off, and never wore it again. The Copycat was exposed, and the Artist was coming alive.

The Artist in a man will clash with the Copycat around him, whether it be in music, style, or zeal for the latest trendy device. He will refuse to do something just to do it, asking the why before joining the hoard of lookalikes.

But even when a man resists the hype and façade of the Copycat, he must also be careful of another imposter. As one squelches the creative energy in the Artist, there is another who would idealize it to the point of fantasy. He can be the ruin of a man, and his name is the Dreamer.

THE DREAMER

Youth will never end, romance is the way of life, every ideal will be reached. These are the beliefs on which the Dreamer floats through life. He and the Hedonist often exist in tandem. While their motives are different, they often achieve the same end.

The Dreamer's rule of life is idealism; his imaginations merge with reality and pull him onward. These unrestrained fantasies eventually take over, blurring the lines between what is real and what is a dream, leaving the Artist far behind.

At the core of the Dreamer is an inability to separate fact from feeling, an unwillingness to ground himself in reality and simply live his life. Dreamers imagine winning the lottery, developing an app that makes a jillion dollars, becoming a YouTube sensation, writing a hit song, landing a book deal, being caught in their moment and going viral. The Dreamer truly believes that he will be that one in a million that strikes proverbial oil, and that on that day his troubles will cease. He often avoids solving the problems in his life because he imagines they will simply vanish once he hits pay dirt. He is sure that he will make his mark on the world, his talent often exaggerated in his own mind.

Dreamers have a need for stimulation and thrill and are quick to jump on the bandwagon of any new thing that excites them – a new style, album, or vocabulary. In their view, things get old quickly and something fresh is needed. The dread of "same old, same old" motivates them to be on the "cutting edge" of what is happening. Always looking to make way for something new and stimulating, they very easily get "used to" anything that seems dated – their clothes, their look, their job, their friends, their spouse.

Because of this, Dreamers are the type who procrastinate, whose check engine light has been on for a good while, who have a list of "I'm gonna" projects that will never be completed. They often quit one thing in order to start another, leaving behind a collection of unfinished ventures - and relationships - in their wake. They make promises to keep people from leaving them, but these promises are hinged on dreams that require others to suspend disbelief. Because of their talent and charisma, Dreamers can sustain the illusion for a time and keep others there with them.

A man characterized by the Dreamer is the type of man who will easily find himself in an adulterous relationship. For him, the drudgery and struggle of his marriage might seem like a dead end, and when he has an opportunity, what appears to be the affair of the century seems like a way out. Because Dreamers live in an alternate, idealistic reality, the consequences of this sort of decision do not seem to have any bearing on their real life. A dreamer will throw away his marriage or gamble away his savings in one night, or ten minutes.

The core defect of the Dreamer is that he has not properly processed disillusionment. Every man will at some point face the death of idealism in his life and have the opportunity to come to terms with it, or not. This is very important. Often we hear of the "midlife crisis," another symptom of this death experience. Put simply, when a man realizes that he cannot buy everything he wants, achieve everything he wants, and have all the sex he wants, he then faces the fact that his youthful idealism is crumbling.

Under the weight of this a man has two choices: either confront the illusion or continue to be led along by it. This illusion is that he is the hero, the unstoppable Adonis, the romantic star of the show that will one day get what is coming to him. The process of disillusionment is just that – we become "dis-illusioned." We realize that what we think of our self and our life, at least in some part, truly *is* an illusion; and we disassociate from it, choosing instead to embrace reality. We spend less time flexing our muscles and perfecting our hairdo in the mirror. At that point we have made progress, but the battle continues – will we accept our new reality and make the best of it or spend the rest of our days sulking over our unaccomplished exploits?

Singer-songwriter Jon Foreman is a beautiful example of an Artist properly handling this struggle. Looking back on his career, he muses: "I have had moments in my life where I've been naïve enough to think I'm going to change the world. And it's a really incredible feeling, the day you discover that's never going to be the case."[6] Here we see it done right: dreams dashed, disillusionment processed, maturity achieved.

When the idealism starts to crumble - whether it be at age thirty or fifty (the earlier, the better) - a man can come to grips with reality and fight off the Dreamer. This makes a man wise. He is able to be himself and nothing more, finding his identity in the proper things. The Artist is in balance, not following the brainwashed multitude nor living in a fantasy. It is then that the best art can come from his life.

THE DECISION TO CREATE LIKE AN ARTIST

We have come to decision number five; will a man…

- pose like a Copycat,
- fantasize like a Dreamer,
- or, like an Artist, *make and enjoy beauty that is transcendent?*

In making this decision, a man must ask himself a few difficult questions:

- Without thinking too deeply, right in this moment, which of these three do I most identify with?
- If asked, how would the people who are closest to me describe me in this regard?

HOMEWORK

Before moving on, take some time (one day or perhaps one week) to ponder the things you have read about the Artist and his imposters. Consider these questions as you interact with this material:

1. In the arenas below, are you a Copycat, a Dreamer, or an Artist?
   a. Work
   b. Marriage, if married; or if not, in a pre-marriage relationship
   c. With my children, if I have any
   d. With my extended family, in-laws, and/or grandchildren
   e. Friendships
   f. Social groups (neighborhood, clubs) and religious groups (church)

2. As you grow in self-awareness, wonder…
   a. Why am I the way I am?
   b. What has positively influenced the Artist in me?
   c. What has led to the takeover of the Copycat or the Dreamer in me?
   d. What past or current life events and memories come to mind as I ask myself these questions?

3. As you think of the future, ponder…
   a. How do I express myself creatively?
   b. If I could create one thing in the next year of my life, what would it be?
   c. What might I remove from my life that would grow the Artist in me?
   d. What specific behaviors might I start practicing or rekindle to this end?

The Mourner

"Welcome all you suckers to Struggleville." [1] - Bill Mallonee

Purpose: *To grieve.*

Decision: *To embrace sorrow as a pathway to growth.*

Much more than just a personality trait or emotional stereotype, the Mourner archetype represents a crucial part of the psyche of a man. Here is a man's ability to grieve, and beyond that, to process sadness and sorrow in such a way that he learns valuable things from them. A man may be depressed and melancholy; however, it is an error to say that this man is a *depressive person*, as if he has no potential beyond that. Perhaps you or I exhibit more of the Mourner than others, but that is not *all* we are, and a man that embraces this quality in a balanced way can benefit much from it.

Mourning is necessary, and this is why the decision to not only grieve but to embrace this process becomes so important in the development of a man. As mentioned in the previous chapter, the death of idealism in a man's life can have crippling effects. When confronted with his limits and faced with the reality that all his hopes and dreams will not come true, many a man becomes permanently disabled. The challenge here is to survive this death, and then experience a rebirth of sorts. The Mourner guides a man on this journey, and while he may acquire a limp along the way, he will be stronger and wiser for it.

THE MOURNER GRIEVES FOR MANY DIFFERENT REASONS

There are many kinds of sorrows that come upon men. Failure is one of the most debilitating. When men experience failure, they begin to question their future. They wonder if they have what it takes any longer. Divorce, job loss, bankruptcy – all of these are common examples.

Men also grieve when they experience tragedy. This includes accident, disability, and illness or death of a loved one. Tragedy also strikes when we lose possessions or relationships.

A third reason for depression in men is the previously-mentioned experience of having our idealism challenged and finding that we come up short. This includes the lack of achievement of one's goals and the realization of one's boundaries. A time comes in a man's life when he wonders "is this as good as it gets?" and when that question lingers, he feels he has no direction or compass.

When these things happen, it is all-important that the Mourner in a man be allowed to do his work. Rather than feign invincibility or sink into his emotions, a man must properly process his grief, and from it press on to maturity.

MOURNERS ARE HONEST ABOUT THEIR SADNESS

The first step of the Mourner developing in a man is that he becomes self-aware enough to be honest with himself about where he is. Admitting one is in a funk is not easy. Often, like the frog in the kettle, we do not realize the gravity of our situation until it is too late.

A Mourner can also be transparent with others, and he has the humility to let on that this is not his best day. Often it takes getting to rock-bottom to admit this, but when that happens it is a good thing. Sometimes the Mourner is birthed when a man realizes that the façades of success and triumph that he presents to others will no longer prop him up.

One of the heroes of the early missions movement is a man by the name of David Brainerd. Centuries ago, young Brainerd left a comfortable life to live in a tent by himself among Native Americans in Connecticut, working to evangelize them and spread the Christian faith. His *Life and Journals of David Brainerd* is one of the most treasured works to come out of this period in the history of evangelical missions.

When one sets out to read these accounts, the expectation might be that of a confident man who shines brightest as a victor, a success story who bravely left his mark. While Brainerd did have remarkable victories and saw a powerful move of God in his short life, the most outstanding theme of his writing is his constant battle with depression.

In his journals, which he submitted to his superiors on a regular basis in order to keep an account of his work and progress, David Brainerd pulled no punches. After declaring an incredible victory on a Sunday, he was often ready to give up on the following Monday. In some of his letters he discusses his hopelessness and thoughts of death; to read them would freeze the blood in your veins. It is a marvel that he was not fetched by his governing board and sent to a mental hospital rather than be allowed to continue in his work as a missionary.

For example, here are a few of Brainerd's thoughts after one pastoral meeting: "Visited another house, where was one dead and laid out; looked on the corpse, and longed that my time might come to depart."[2] This sort of narrative is the norm, not the exception, in his accounts. The sobriety of these writings is a model of the healthy balance of the Mourner alive in a man, demonstrating that he can be all at once defeated and victorious.

THE MOURNER ACCEPTS THAT THERE WILL BE TROUBLE

John Bunyan, writing from a jail cell where he was imprisoned because of his preaching, said it well. "The wise God will have it so: some will pipe, and some must weep."[3] Here we have a man in prison properly mourning; in the very midst of his trouble, he acknowledges that there is some providence even in his miserable situation. It is the swallowing of the reality of suffering that makes the meal more digestible.

We find another example of such endurance in the legacy of Samuel Rutherford, another Christian minister of old. A beacon of hope to those experiencing hardship, Rutherford's letters talk much of his personal experiences. The tragic loss of several children, betrayal by friends, imprisonment for his faith – these were just the beginnings of his miseries. The Mourner shows up often in his writings, speaking of an acceptance of the trials that rightly come upon anyone trying to walk in the narrow way. He writes, "The Lord sent Paul on many errands where he found lions in his way. It is folly to think to steal to heaven with a whole skin."[4]

THE MOURNER SITS IN HIS DISCOMFORT AND LETS IT SHAPE HIM

If a man must first accept his difficulties, his next task is to embrace them. This is not some archaic masochism at work – rather it really is what "separates the men from the boys." I once heard that the difference between the first world and the third world is this: In the first world, people experience difficulty and find a way to remove it from their life; whereas in the third world, people experience difficulty and find a way to adapt to it. Storyteller Gene Edwards says it this way: "God is looking for men who will live in pain."[5]

If it is possible to cut our mourning and misery short, so be it. But often it is not possible, and in these times the Mourner stops kicking against the proverbial goads and accepts his situation. The longer we push back against something that will not change, the more miserable we become. Some men go to the grave still pushing.

The knee-jerk reaction when we see a person suffering is to pat them on the back, tell them it will be okay, and say trite things in an attempt to sidestep the awkwardness of their pain. The truth is that in this life we will not always be completely healed, and there is no medicine for certain maladies. Telling a person who has lost a loved one that they will one day "get over it" – as if that were possible – is the opposite of helpful.

Once I heard a sad man singing a dirge; the lyrics were,

> *"All you can do with your suffering is suffer through*
> *Sooner or later pain will find its way right back to you.*
> *But it will be alright at the breaking of the day*
> *When the breaking of the night forever fades away."* [6]

The Mourner understands this, both in others and in himself, and becomes content to simply suffer and let the process of suffering do its work. When offering sympathy to others in need, in the same vein, the Mourner can compassionately listen and let his listening be the only comfort he dares to give.

MOURNERS ACCEPT HARD TIMES WITHOUT BLAMING OTHERS

When we speak of providence and tragedy, we must also recognize that sometimes difficulties befall those who seem the least deserving of them. A few relevant Old Testament musings on this topic: "I have seen slaves on horseback and princes walking on foot like slaves...I envied the arrogant when I saw the prosperity of the wicked. They have no struggles; their bodies are healthy and strong. They are free from common human burdens; they are not plagued by human ills."[7]

This is the truth; sometimes justice does not prevail this side of heaven. Swallowing that is difficult, and if a man is not careful, this incongruity will leave him permanently vexed. Much of our trouble with this reality is that we don't believe we are deserving of suffering, but rather that we can somehow avoid it by making the right choices and having what we might call good luck or good karma. But this is not the case, especially for someone who claims to believe in God. How often those who claim Jesus as their master wish for all the glory but none of the cross.

Taking this further, if one can bear it, there are times in the journey of faith when evil and suffering are purposely placed in our path for some sovereign purpose. This is an advanced lesson and one that few men imagine in the realm of possibility within which their faith functions. Consider the story of poor Job. Satan did not find him; rather, *it was God that pointed him out* to Satan and suggested that he be tested.

The language in the Bible, in terms of describing God's dealing with his faithful, is often offensive to our view of some grandfatherly deity that exists to make us happy. No; instead, he chops us, clubs us, burns us, devours us, and destroys us. John the Baptist, called the greatest in the kingdom of heaven, died doubting in a prison cell, his head removed from him because a drunken politician was turned on by a spoiled bimbo. Jesus' take on John's undeserving fate? "Blessed is the one who isn't offended by this."[8]

One of the more riveting meetings I have had with God happened when I first discovered Judges chapter 20, a passage I would summarize with the words "when God sends you to die."[9] Were most supposed God-fearing people to read this and incorporate it into their first-world faith, I wonder if they would still believe. Sometimes I wonder if I really do. Lord, I believe; help my unbelief.

It is in these types of trials that a man needs the Mourner most. This archetype can experience pain, no matter how it originates, and process it in a way that helps him move forward rather than freezing or falling back. Surviving a difficulty without placing the blame on man or on God, but rather trusting in a higher wisdom and providence than we can understand, takes us far down the path of the maturing Mourner.

THE MOURNER RECOGNIZES GRIEF AS A SACRED THING

Somewhere in our grief there is a treasure. If we can survive it, sorrow gives us a glimpse into the pain of others, allowing us to express sympathy and offer comfort. It allows us to see the bigger picture of life, and it grows appreciation in us for what we do have. It is said that youth is wasted on the young. We do not often realize the blessing of our health until it is taken from us. We do not appreciate the comforts we have until they are gone.

Beyond making us more sympathetic and grateful, sorrow opens our eyes to divine forces at work in the universe. In his short book *Lament for a Son*, Nicholas

Wolterstorff grapples with the death of his 25-year-old son in an accident. His observations on the interaction between his tragedy and his faith are those of the Mourner: "Through the prism of my tears I have seen a suffering God. It is said of God that no one can behold his face and live. I always thought this meant that no one can see his splendor and live. A friend said perhaps it meant that no one could see his sorrow and live. Or perhaps his sorrow is splendor."[10]

THE MOURNER SEES BITTERNESS AS A DOORWAY TO SOMETHING SWEETER

Going even further, this sacredness, in the divine economy, can usher sweetness into our lives. By now we have seen that this progression in the Mourner is possible: from sorrow to acceptance, from acceptance to embracing, from embracing to sacredness, and now from sacredness to sweetness.

A prime example of this evolution is found in the life of Jesus. In the garden of Gethsemane it is recorded that Jesus is sorrowful to the point of death. Despite that, he accepts his situation, surrendering to what providence has dictated for his life. From that moment on he embraces his impending death, doing nothing to resist as he is falsely tried, tortured, and crucified. We see a rich sacredness in his final moments as he forgives and shows compassion to those who hate him. The end of it all is sweetness. "For the joy set before him he endured the cross."[11] On the other end of this experience, the outcome for the Son of God was joy.

A man who knows how to mourn can, like Jesus, endure hardship because he anticipates that there will be some redemptive joy on the other side of suffering. Bunyan, writing from the vantage point of a small child, speaks to this. When asked what he might think when circumstances come upon him that he does not understand, he replies:

"The bitter must come before the sweet, and that also will make the sweet the sweeter."[12] Hundreds of years earlier, St. Augustine said the same thing differently: "Everywhere the greater joy is ushered in by the greater pain."[13]

THERE ARE SOME LESSONS THAT ONLY THE MOURNER CAN TEACH

A man who has reached adulthood knows well that he has a perspective which until that time he could not understand. One who has gone to war sees the world differently than one who has not. A married man has learned things about life and love that no single man understands, and a father has an understanding far more broad than a man who has never sired children. This is not to say that one is in some way less than the other, but it does stand that some life lessons can only be learned through experiencing them.

The same is true for mourning, and this is the greatest gift that the Mourner can give to a man. He who has learned to mourn properly has a depth to him that can be acquired no other way. Until one has stood through the storms of life and come out of them, still alive, even smiling, he cannot give others guidance to weather the same. For this reason, Mourners are rare. The majority of men flunk out of the school of mourning and learn other things from their pain such as pretending and sulking. But the man who embraces his sorrow comes out of it richer, more steady, and ready to offer comfort to others.

There is a man from whom I learned much of the ways of the Mourner some years ago. I had known this man as an acquaintance; as we lived on opposite coasts, I only saw him on occasion during work-related regional meetings. I had once given him a ride to the airport at which time we talked briefly. He was the pastor of a large and well-known church in my denomination and had some level of international notoriety.

Because of this, it became widely known when tragedy struck his life unexpectedly. Within two days his three-year-old son went from healthy to ill, and then suddenly passed away. His world fell apart; a man who had answers for everyone suddenly had none for himself.

A few years later, I saw him at a week-long conference. Or rather, he saw me: I was alone in the dining hall early one morning when he entered the room, filled up his plate with southern fare, and scanned the room for a breakfast partner. Before long we were talking.

Skipping the formalities, I began asking questions. This was a season in my life that was quite trying; I was in the midst of the worst of my daughter's health challenges that I described two chapters earlier. I shared my story, describing the years of struggle, the hospitals, the surgeries, the loneliness, the pain of normal life lost. After a long story made short, I dared to dig deep, looking for some sort of advice on how to weather this storm. I concluded my brief autobiography with a question: "How did *you* survive your tragedy?" His answer was unexpected: "We didn't."

No more needed to be said. Obviously, he was still going, still married, still working, still eating bacon and eggs even. The point was that he did not need to surmount his mourning and grief in order to move on. Rather, *it became part of him*, shaping him. He worked through it, accepted it as a new part of his life, and went forward willing to carry it rather than deny it or medicate the pain. The Mourner spoke those two words and did not try to explain them; they just hung in the nearly empty room and sunk deep into my soul.

Sorrow will come upon us all. It might stay briefly or painfully linger for a long time. Whether it be tragedy, disillusionment, or some other type of crushing experience, a man will face his limits as the weight of these crushes his soul. It is in such times that the Mourner is most important. When a man processes defeat in a healthy way, he grows in wisdom and is able to help others who face the same battles.

But the temptation for the Mourner to be bypassed is great, perhaps greater than with any of the other archetypes. When a man stifles his need to grieve, his soul hardens and he becomes the Mannequin. Conversely, if he over-identifies with his depression and chooses to wallow in his misery, he finds himself on an endless spiral inward, a path taken by the narcissistic imposter known as the Sulk.

THE MANNEQUIN

In the early twentieth century, the manufacturing world was revolutionized by the advent of a new invention. Until this product arrived on the scene, most things were made of metal, which had to be recovered from ore; or stone, which had to be baked; or wood, which had to be grown. Everything changed when these natural resources were in large part replaced by a synthetic substance known as plastic.

Plastic truly is an amazing thing. It is lightweight, highly resistant to corrosion and chemicals, and has a very low thermal conductivity. It is resistant to shock, durable, and relatively inexpensive to manufacture. Plastic is used to make cars, houses, and toys; it goes underwater and into outer space. It can be formed into virtually any shape needed and comes in a wide range of colors.

At some point, plastic began being used to make human dolls known as mannequins. I remember when I was a little boy, walking through the shopping mall, and I first laid my eyes on a mannequin. It was creepy and

107

wonderful at the same time; even attractive in some macabre way. At some point, I ventured to touch the wrist of one and was startled (why, I don't know; when you are seven, things are often like this) to feel something cold and hard instead of human.

This is a parable of what can happen if a man allows the Mannequin to subvert the mourning process in his life. He might look human, but get near him and you will discover something very plasticky and fake. The denial of the proper process of grief and mourning causes a crust to develop over the soul. While the "fake it till you make it" strategy has some merit, the use of this survival mechanism for a prolonged period of time can have devastating effects.

To refuse the journey into our grief is a type of denial. When we do this we deny ourselves the opportunity to experience life and the pain it brings. We pick and choose what we accept, as if in life we were the master of our own destiny. Seeking to maintain control, when anything too disagreeable comes along, we manage a dour composure and become like a mannequin – cold and hard – in an attempt to withstand the powerful forces that are eroding us. We refuse to accept that we will be changed by pain and therefore lose some of our humanity as a result.

This refusal takes many forms. I have witnessed people completely deny their part in the dissolution of a relationship, as if it was entirely caused by the other person. Another will not take their obviously handicapped child in for evaluation because they cannot accept the stigma of a diagnosis. Another laid in a hospice bed, his skin turned green and yellow, denying that cancer existed in his body and was bringing his life to an end.

Back once again to this expression: "Stop kicking against the goads." It originates from the propensity of oxen or other animals used for plowing to kick back against the sharp stick used to prod them onward. A reaction to the pain of goading makes the animal resist surrender to something greater than it – a human who is calling the shots. In the same way, mourning takes humility and surrender. We have to let the goads draw blood and do their work, and then we must surrender so that the field can be plowed. To rebel against this process does a man much harm and installs the Mannequin in his life. Bleeding, stubborn, full of pretension, devoid of humility, this faker is the ruin of not only a man but also the good fruit of maturity and resolve that would grow in his garden.

But the Mannequin is not the only replacement available for this archetype. The over-emphasis of the Mourner in a man's life invites an invader who is very different but just as destructive. He is common among men today, and his name is the Sulk.

THE SULK

When a man mourns but his sadness is not kept in check, the Sulk is right around the corner, ready to provide unlimited amounts of Kleenexes. Men degenerate into this milksop because they are unwilling to deal with difficulty and offense. Instead, they revert to a previous "save point" in their life, that of an adolescent or even toddler, and that is the level of emotional maturity with which they face struggle. In some cases men do not regress as such because there is no regression needed. These men have never grown past that level of coping and effortlessly assume the necessary pouty expression and puerile behavior by which they plan to garner coddling as the situation dictates.

The Sulk is a diabolical enemy of manhood; his sappy influence on the other archetypes in man causes an ineffectiveness or even impotence as he attempts to fight, lead, love, or laugh. Many men identify with him as their primary surrogate for life each day from the time they wake until they go to sleep. They might even begin the morning happy and refreshed, but quickly remember to assume the temperament of the Sulk before getting too far into the day.

Such men even choose depression, subconsciously assuming the role of critic and complainer in most situations that they find challenging. Interestingly, men who sulk are often characterized by a mixture of both obsessive sadness and brooding anger. A man of this nature is touchy; people tend to be aware of his propensity to mope and brood, and feel they have to walk on eggshells around him. He is unable to be approached about his emotional stunting without exploding in anger or, still worse, going into a deeper bout of sulking.

For this reason, people tend to maintain distance from the Sulk. His cleverly crafted barricades to any constructive criticism help keep him in a pit of narcissism, which is exactly where he wants to be. Those who are close to him are often enablers of his behavior and tend to be Sulks themselves. Tissues for our tears can stunt our growth. The very worst thing to do when a Sulk is sulking is to displace his sadness with tissues. Often, people just need to cry and snot all over themselves and deal with it.

When a man is personified by the Sulk, moodiness mixed with a propensity to anger means that he is easily offended; typically, he keeps a mental list on hand of certain types of people or behaviors that he deems "annoying." He moans and gripes about the same things week in and week out; he just can't believe this is this way and that is that way. Commenting on this decay of manhood, Robert Bly describes such conduct well: "If he feels hurt, or in a low mood, he identifies with the mood, and everyone around him has to go down into the hole."[14]

If the Sulk is allowed to continue on in a man, he slowly but surely becomes isolated and bitter, his melancholy completing its work in redefining him. He sees life as unfair, evaluating and comparing himself to "how it should be" or "what I thought it would be like" or "what everyone else has." This causes him to be mean and critical, unable to love others and express much sympathy toward their plight without quickly refocusing the pity on himself. In the end, his life is one big pity party to which he invites as many as will come; the order of business has the attendees stroking and babying him such that he remains stuck in a perpetual cycle of petulant bellyaching.

THE DECISION TO GRIEVE LIKE A MOURNER

We have come to decision number six; will a man…

- fake it like a Mannequin,
- mope like a Sulk,
- or, like a Mourner, *embrace sorrow as a pathway to growth?*

In making this decision, a man must ask himself a few difficult questions:

- Without thinking too deeply, right in this moment, which of these three do I most identify with?
- If asked, how would the people who are closest to me describe me in this regard?

HOMEWORK

Before moving on, take some time (one day or perhaps one week) to ponder the things you have read about the Mourner and his imposters. Consider these questions as you interact with this material:

1. In the arenas below, are you a Mannequin, a Sulk, or a Mourner?
   a. Work
   b. Marriage, if married; or if not, in a pre-marriage relationship
   c. With my children, if I have any
   d. With my extended family, in-laws, and/or grandchildren
   e. Friendships
   f. Social groups (neighborhood, clubs) and religious groups (church)

2. As you grow in self-awareness, wonder…
    a. Why am I the way I am?
    b. What has positively influenced the Mourner in me?
    c. What has led to the takeover of the Mannequin or the Sulk in me?
    d. What past or current life events and memories come to mind as I ask myself these questions?

3. As you think of the future, ponder…
    a. What am I grieving right now in the season I find myself in?
    b. What might I learn from this experience that will grow my soul?
    c. What might I remove from my life that would grow the Mourner in me?
    d. What specific behaviors might I start practicing or rekindle to this end?

The Wizard

"*For but few things are there, which we speak properly, most things improperly.*" [1] – St. Augustine

Purpose: *To learn.*

Decision: *To humbly learn as much as possible and pass the same on to others.*

A Wizard in his purest form is, according to the etymology of the word, a wise person. What the word *wise* actually means will be discussed below in depth. But let us begin by saying that this archetype represents the part of a man that is willing to learn, has learned, and as a result can dispense this learning to others.

While the Wizard certainly might be thought of as a

sage, the latter term is less appropriate for this discussion because sages are old and gray, but Wizards can be very young. Scripture tells us that "a poor yet wise lad is better than an old and foolish king who no longer knows how to receive instruction."[2] So an old man can be a fool and a young boy can be known for wisdom. A life of wizarding can and should begin before the hair on our head either grays or falls out.

The Wizard might occupy the role of judge, professor, or coach. He lives in anyone who has something decent to say that comes from a place of temperance and study. The Wizard is crucial to a man's development because it is this archetype that, as he ages, makes him a person of substance. A man inhabited by the Wizard is known less for what he does and more for who he is. This type of depth comes only from a humble and lifelong posture of learning. Because of this quality, a man can have tremendous influence on others; the older and more learned he becomes, the more he can give away.

WIZARDS ARE KNOWN FOR KNOWING THINGS WORTH KNOWING

When you think of a Wizard, it is likely that you think of a very old man, girded in a flowing robe, a gnarly staff in his bony hand, a long white beard flowing off his face and into the wind. This stereotype exists largely because of fiction literature that has emerged in the last few centuries. While this depiction of the Wizard is somewhat accurate, the title of "wizard" actually means more.

The word has its roots in medieval times; it comes from the phrase, "wise'ard." The root of the first word is *wys*, meaning 'wise'. The next part of this word, *-ard*, is designated as the second part of many titles, along with *-art*, and as such is often used as an intensifier. The coward was known for cowing, the braggart was known for bragging, the drunkard for being drunk. In the same manner, the *wizard* was known for his wisdom – he had something to say that came from a deep place, and when he spoke, people turned to listen.

WIZARDS ARE LESS SMART AND MORE TEACHABLE

For this study, we again consult what is regarded as the greatest manual for wisdom in print, the Proverbs of the Old Testament. I have read this part of the Bible over a hundred times. In my first few dozen times through, I thought that I was perusing a collection of right and accurate sayings about various topics in life. Love, money, friendship, conflict resolution, and more are discussed; there is so much to read and apply to one's life there. At some point, as I read and re-read these ancient scriptures, I began to notice a theme, and I suddenly realized that I had it all wrong. For so long I thought that wisdom was the collecting of truth and the ability to live and dispense it. While that is one definition of wisdom, the purest definition of wisdom is quite different.

Simply put, true wisdom is *the ability to receive instruction*. There is a big difference between knowing things and being willing to learn things. A person who knows a lot can be an utter fool if he is not able to learn. Learning is what defines the Wizard, not knowledge. Knowledge comes from learning, but it is a teachable heart that makes a person wise.

Back to the Proverbs - we find this theme woven throughout the book, so much so that it is easy to gloss over it because it is reiterated so often. Wisdom is shouting for us to listen, accept reproof, and grow. A few examples: "A wise man *will hear* and increase in learning. *Heed instruction* and become wise. The wise in heart will *receive commands*. A wise man is he who *listens to counsel*. He who *regards reproof* is prudent. *Listen to counsel and accept discipline* that you may be wise the rest of your days."[3] There is an intrinsic connection between a man's ability to be taught and the presence of wisdom in his life.

So, the question is not about what you know, nor how many college degrees you have, nor what your life experiences have been. Rather, the question that determines if a man has the Wizard living in him is: *Are you teachable?* This question is a beautiful invitation into something that will deepen us if we take the bait. Once this issue is settled, the Wizard can begin growing in a man.

WIZARDS ARE KEENLY AWARE OF HOW LITTLE THEY KNOW ABOUT ANYTHING

The beginning of wisdom is humility - a humility which can admit that in our strength we are still weak, in our riches we are still poor, at our very best we are still fools blindly trying to navigate a vast world. The Wizard has experienced both the bigness of the universe and the smallness of his self. When the two are coupled and this coupling is thought on for even a moment, a deep sobriety is produced in a man's soul.

This modest posture invites the Wizard and staves off the temptation to pride that so easily comes upon a man and prohibits him from growing. We as a human race are quite full of ourselves and tend to disregard the tested and true voices of age and wisdom. The new college graduate receives his diploma and is certain he is about to do something that has never been done. The new husband feels such unstoppable affection for his bride that he is sure they will never "fall out of love." The new parent has studied the latest childrearing techniques, believes them to be superior to what the previous generation did, and is convinced that the aging parents of that time are irrelevant. The new pastor, saddled with a bag of hip and novel tricks he'll use to grow a church and reach the next generation, storms forward with little thought of the millennia of tradition on which he builds.

Because of our pride and want for attention, we tend

to showcase our understanding of things as if we really know *something*. Imagine a large white wall, perhaps in an auditorium, reaching far in every direction, up to the ceiling. Now imagine if we were to take an ink pen and place a small black dot somewhere on the wall. This represents the knowledge you or I might possess in relation to everything else that we do not. Our tendency is to point to that one dot, on the backdrop of all else, and passionately focus the attention of everyone onto just how much we know. In contrast, a Wizard sees the wall, not the ink spot, and speaks and acts accordingly.

This is what St. Augustine meant in his statement referenced at the opening of this chapter. Once another wise man, having returned from another world and experiencing the wonders there, was heard to have said that there were a thousand things right around him on earth that he knew absolutely nothing about. In this same search for humility, C.S. Lewis muses, "We must keep always before our eyes that vision in which God carried in his hand a little object like a nut, and that nut was 'all that was made.' "[4]

WIZARDS VALUE SUBSTANCE OVER SIZE
Building on this humility, the Wizard is unimpressed by the accumulation of knowledge, money, power, and accomplishment. He understands that the text of every book in the local library and more can be stored on a hard drive the size of his fingernail. Instead of thirsting for knowledge, he values substance.

When a Wizard speaks, his words have weight because they are first tried before being spoken. There is a line in an old Hebrew song in which the words of God are described as perfect, like silver that is tested seven times in a furnace.[5] A Wizard has heard this tune and, wishing to emulate such excellence, thinks over his statement seven times before speaking. Instead of adding to the deluge of disposable conversation happening around him, he chooses not to say everything that occurs to him; therefore, when he does speak, it means something. Like renowned trumpet player Miles Davis said, "You have to know four hundred notes you can play, then pick the right four."[6]

In any organization or social group, quality suffers in proportion to growth. This is not necessarily a bad thing, but at some point we must ask if the proper balance between the two is fulfilling our vision. Do we sacrifice our vision in order to grow? Recognizing the value of substance over size, the Wizard asks this question. Sometimes the answer leads to a choice to plateau or even downsize, a decision counter to most organizational models in which "bigger is better" is the order of the day.

One could learn much of the Wizard in studying the Jesuit movement. Its founder, Ignatius of Loyola, was blissfully unconcerned about the badgering of his superiors to keep accounts and systematize his dreams. Instead of going where he could find the largest crowds, he would instead walk all day, barefoot, to a city where he knew one person with which to converse about his faith.[7]

WIZARDS TAKE THE LONG VIEW ON THINGS
The Wizard is able to be patient. His palate prefers a slow-cooked stew to a microwaved can of soup. This is why, as was said earlier, the further along a Wizard goes, the more he has to offer. The archetype we are discussing is less a hip spell-caster and more an aging and weathered one. His soul is seasoned over time, and like a good meal marinating over a wood fire, the aroma he gives off is strong and savory.

Let us again consider Ignatius; profound lessons abound. You would not notice this until you studied his various works and considered a timeline of when each was written, but it was not until he was in his fifties and sixties that he even began drafting what would become his most famous writings. In a world where the age of forty is a death sentence, it is hard to imagine that a person's peak output would happen when our culture deems them invalid and unable to contribute, but that is often the case. The Wizard does not see his growing age as a proportional gauge to his loss of influence; if anything, he sees the opposite dynamic at work. He is farsighted, taking the long view of life and his part in it.

THE WIZARD IS APPRENTICED BY ANOTHER WIZARD

We only have as much authority as we are willing to be under. In their youth, Gandalf looked to Saruman, and Kenobi looked to Yoda. In the same way, in order to learn, a man must look to others from whom he can receive coaching and mentorship. This is another expression of humility in the life of the Wizard, that he is able to place himself under the counsel of others.

The presence of mentors in a man's life is critical for his survival. These relationships occur in a variety of ways; a man might have a planned arrangement, such as a coach or counselor with whom he meets regularly. Another method of apprenticeship is the commitment to self-study. Wizards have extensive libraries filled with many books - the older the books, the better. A man said once that he found his best counselors in the graveyard; by this he meant that it was through the writings of many classic authors that he had learned much. Time-tested truth packs a punch.

Whatever his need is for instruction, the Wizard is willing to ask for assistance from others. This is why the teenage years tend to be a low point for Wizard development in a man. As a boy becomes a man he must differentiate from his parents and younger self and then molt in a sense, shedding the old boy and becoming a young man. This process involves him taking on responsibility and carving out a path of his own destiny. The emotional tumult that accompanies the years of puberty often causes young men to shun all counsel; this leaves them no choice but to learn things the hard way. If they recover the ability to be taught by others, they develop into men. Sadly, some men - even gray-haired men - are still raging against the system like a teenager, the Wizard nowhere to be found.

WIZARDS ARE NOT ALWAYS RIGHT AND THEY KNOW IT

As we speak of this character, we must address one more issue. Critical to his development is the ability to receive admonishing from others. It is one thing to learn from a book or a classroom, but a whole other thing to have another human offer rebuke. A wise man has trusted people in his life who have access to do just that when needed. Nobody goes very long without needing some sort of gentle correction.

In order to grow in wisdom, men must make themselves accountable to others. This means that from time to time they will be told things about themselves that they do not want to hear. The Wizard is able to listen, without becoming defensive or fighting back, and consider the correction given to him. This is the most transformative part of being mentored; it is easy to receive encouragement and coaching, but the best growth happens when others dare to speak into our lives in such a way that might cause us to temporarily nosedive due to the challenge being presented. We need trusted friends in our lives to point out our blind spots. Whether we can humbly receive these corrections without becoming indignant or rebellious is the litmus test that will determine if we will grow. The fool will not recognize his folly and only continues in it; in contrast, the wise man hears and course-corrects accordingly.

WIZARDS POUR THEMSELVES INTO OTHERS

For the Wizard, the mentoring relationship occurs in two directions. He always has someone (or something) in front of him that he is following, and he always has someone behind him that he is leading. He might do this in an official role; perhaps as a teacher, counselor, or trainer. Or he might function as a mentor unofficially, being someone that people naturally seek out for wisdom and guidance. Either way, the Wizard is always ready to help others, and even proactive in finding avenues to do so.

In this regard, men who embrace this archetype have a scrappiness about them. There is a reality that, as men advance toward retirement age, they become less interested in the work that was once required of them. This is normal and is part of the reward of living a long and productive life. The time comes when we can sleep in more, work less, and experience the dusk of our lives doing things we enjoy. At the same time there is a responsibility to stay fresh and sharp, remaining available for those coming up behind us. We may not work as much in our older age, but we have a mantle on us that we must proactively pass onto others.

Consider the two heroes mentioned earlier, Gandalf and Obi-wan Kenobi. One of the most memorable parts of their legacies is the moment in their stories when they, the aged Wizard, pull out a sword and fiercely fight the enemy. I remember many years ago as a boy watching these men in action. For much of their screen time they simply bumbled about and said profound things; but as the battle climaxed, they unsheathed their weapon and engaged - and heads rolled. The modern-day Wizard chooses to remain involved in the lives and battles of others. Rather than retire to the recliner, he instead keeps the cobwebs from growing on him and stays present along the journey of other younger men who need his guidance. Old and haggard, but still ever ready to fight – the Wizard alive and well.

At the young age of nineteen I wandered into a church for the first time of my life. I had recently discovered religion on my own, and thanks to the prodding of a friend with whom I worked at a fast-food restaurant, I found a place where other people who were seeking God could meet and experience him.

In my time with those people, many of them came beside me, filling the role of father that was missing in my life. There was one man in this group that had a most profound impact on me; he was the pastor of the church. I had the privilege of informally sitting under him for about a decade, learning everything I could. As I think of the qualities of this first mentor in my adult life, those of the Wizard were most outstanding in him. He was incredibly bold and fearless, but at the same time he could be incredibly gentle. It is rare to see that balance in a man, and in this case it kept me continually inspired, for I wanted to be like this as well.

Once, after conducting a dynamic meeting that saw hundreds moved, crying, and laid out all over the floor, a few of us were in the parking lot, preparing to go our separate ways. A new member of the church approached, an older man, and began to sing the praises of the pastor, declaring his loyalty and commitment to the church and his leadership. My mentor must have seen something because without hesitation he said "We will see if I am your pastor when I have to tell you no." Only a short time after that the man showed his true colors, attempting a coup d'état. He was unable to serve and desired only to lead, which caused him to leave the fellowship in the worst way, blaming God and everyone else as he did. His takeover attempt resulted in nothing but bitterness in his heart.

In stark contrast to this was the mentor of whom I am speaking. In my years with him, he took me along to many conferences, both out of state and out of the country, as a travel partner. We jogged together, shared hotel rooms, and flew across the ocean. In these contexts over many years I saw him brush his teeth, drink plenty of coffee, and deal with loss, criticism, tragedy, and many other difficulties. In these battles I watched him, a Wizard, seek out many other Wizards for comfort and guidance.

Even into his older age he never disengaged from the learning process, whether it involved God or man being the teacher. At every church service, conference, and seminar, most of which he led, he remained in a constant posture of receiving. I watched him a hundred times conversing with others, and most of what he did was listen, but when he did talk there was tremendous power to his words. Typically, before the speaking part of the liturgy there is an extended time of corporate worship. This man never failed to engage, quietly singing, arms open wide, often kneeling or prostrate, unconcerned about reviewing his speaking notes, lost in the moment.

I will always remember this scene in my mind. Now that I am in his shoes, leading a church and serving as a model for others, I am sure that many are watching me. Will I be the professional type, aloof and disengaged from people in the hurriedness of my responsibility? Will I be known as highbrow, emanating an air of superiority because of my position? Or will I be a shepherd who smells like his sheep, a general who sleeps on the field with his troops; still humble, still learning, still available?

I am grateful for such a model of the Wizard in my life. I saw what a man looks like when he takes this path, and because of his example I can emulate the same, and lead others there too. It is my aim to remain a student as long as I am breathing, no matter how many people are looking to me to be the teacher.

Following in the way of the Wizard brings a powerful quality to a man. By walking in this path, he becomes a life-long learner, embracing humility and willing to ask for help. At the same time, he is able to lead others as he has been led, offering guidance and mentorship along the way. He is an example of the sacred wisdom so needed in our day.

But if a man repeatedly refuses the opportunity that guidance and correction offer him, he will quickly take a wayward detour. A man who ignores the learning process in life shrinks into the Simpleton; he who values learning but does not embrace humility looks down upon others with the obtuse glare of the Know-it-all.

THE SIMPLETON

A Simpleton is just that – a simple man, but not in the sense of being plain. Rather, he is simple in the sense that he is unlearned because he chooses not to be taught. Simpletons are content to function on an elementary level that is far lower than their capacity. Sometimes it is laziness that leads to this complacency, and other times it is apathy.

When a man is a Simpleton, he has no depth. The cost of getting out a shovel and searching for the proverbial gold in life is too high for his low level of emotional stamina. Rather, he wades in the shallows, always taking the path of least resistance rather than choosing the risk inherent in pursuing some new adventure.

When a Simpleton is challenged, he is so thick-headed that even the soundest wisdom will not get through to him. He cannot even learn from his own mistakes; if given the opportunity, he will rush headlong into the same errors he has already committed. The Proverbs once again: "A rebuke goes deeper into one who has understanding than a hundred blows into a fool. Though you pound him in a mortar with a pestle, yet his folly will not depart from him. Like a dog that returns to its vomit, he again repeats his folly."[8]

This behavior perpetuates itself in the Simpleton, which is why even a hundred blows will accomplish nothing. The perceived cost of changing his ways is too high, so the beatings continue, and the Simpleton is just fine with that. He would rather remain anonymous and have nothing required of him than give in to the pressure being put on him to change.

This is at the heart of what makes a man choose the Simpleton over the Wizard: the refusal to change. In our study of the Wizard we discovered that one of his key qualities is being teachable, and that whatever lesson is learned necessitates adjustment in such a man. This might require him to alter his speech, spending, or quite possibly the entire paradigm from which he lives.

The Simpleton refuses this change because with it comes new responsibility. If he makes himself accountable to a higher standard by learning something new, he must then "service what he sells." The Simpleton wishes to be responsible for nothing and therefore aspires to nothing.

The end result for a man who chooses this path is one of naiveté; he blends into the background, ignorant, unable to contribute to things that require thinking and effort. People who are forced to be in his proximity have mostly given up on him, allocating the Simpleton to a place in their life where he can cause the least amount of damage and need the least amount of guidance. The Simpleton is content being a cog in the wheel, for there he is unnoticed. This is exactly what he wants, and from this posture he lives his life out in a very hollow and inconsequential way.

The Simpleton is a stale alternative to the Wizard. But there is another enemy of this archetype that is birthed when a man overemphasizes learning to his hurt. When a man becomes educated but does so without the added ingredients of humility and transparency, the Know-it-all struts into his life.

THE KNOW-IT-ALL

Opposite to the Simpleton we have the Know-it-all. Rather than get out of the way, this mockery of humble manhood stands firmly where he can be seen by as many observers as is possible, ready to dispense his professed wisdom to all. He finds his identity in his intellect and knowledge, often using it to shame others and build himself up by comparison.

There is a scene in the film *Good Will Hunting* that depicts this well. Matt Damon plays Will, a janitor with hidden genius, who has had enough of a Know-it-all graduate student who is using his intellect to embarrass others who are not as bright. A confrontation ensues in which the student quotes several authors in order to impress the small crowd gathered around. Will puts him in his place, cutting him off and completing each quote from memory, at the same time exposing his opponents' lack of original thought. The entire scene serves as a powerful contrast between the humble scholarship of the Wizard and the arrogance of this imposter.[9]

And it is arrogance that defines such a man as this. He loves having those he labels his disciples nearby, their admiration pumping up his sense of worth; their need for his approval fulfilling his own secret need for their approval. Those who do not qualify to be his pupils are ignored, while those who might challenge or match him at some level are deemed unworthy of his attention and treated as insignificant. He is all at once aloof, imperious, and snooty; were he an animal he would be a large peacock, proudly pecking here and there, his full plumage on display.

When it comes to accountability, the Know-it-all has none. He sets his own standards, believing himself to be the final and best-informed authority on any matter. Men like this are dangerous in power. When given any level of authority - heaven forbid it be absolute - they grossly misuse it. Know-it-alls will even bend rules to their benefit because they sincerely believe that things would work better if they were in control. Morality is not important to them; only achievement.

The Know-it-all, like the Mogul and the Brute, tends to live a lonely life. His behavior creates for him a place of near isolation, surrounded only by the few people that match his level of pomp and propriety. Secretly, he also believes himself to be above each of these, which is why Know-it-alls often shoot their own. Those that are left are only still around because the Know-it-all enjoys their constant pining for his decrees and control over their lives. He keeps them ever coming back for more, feeding his ego, perpetuating his sense of self-importance, and keeping him immune from growing in any true wisdom.

THE DECISION TO LEARN LIKE A WIZARD
We have come to decision number seven; will a man...

- ignore like a Simpleton,
- snub like a Know-it-all,
- or, like a Wizard, *humbly learn as much as possible and pass the same on to others?*

In making this decision, a man must ask himself a few difficult questions:

- Without thinking too deeply, right in this moment, which of these three do I most identify with?
- If asked, how would the people who are closest to me describe me in this regard?

HOMEWORK
Before moving on, take some time (one day or perhaps one week) to ponder the things you have read about the Wizard and his imposters. Consider these questions as you interact with this material:

1. In the arenas below, are you a Simpleton, a Know-it-all, or a Wizard?
   a. Work
   b. Marriage, if married; or if not, in a pre-marriage relationship
   c. With my children, if I have any
   d. With my extended family, in-laws, and/or grandchildren
   e. Friendships
   f. Social groups (neighborhood, clubs) and religious groups (church)

2.   As you grow in self-awareness, wonder…
   a. Why am I the way I am?
   b. What and who has positively influenced the Wizard in me?
   c. What has led to the takeover of the Simpleton or the Know-it-all in me?
   d. What past or current life events and memories come to mind as I ask myself these questions?

3.   As you think of the future, ponder…
   a. Who are the people in my life that have served as positive mentors and coaches?
   b. What am I learning right now? What would I like to learn?
   c. Who do I have some level of influence over that might benefit from my guidance?
   d. What might I remove from my life that would grow the Wizard in me?
   e. What specific behaviors might I start practicing or rekindle to this end?

The Mystic

"Just now I was higher than the sky." [1] – Ignatius of Loyola

Purpose: *To ascend.*

Decision: *To devote oneself to God and experience the things beyond.*

The Mystic represents the man that is imbued with the very presence of God. Though placed at the end in our study, this archetype is the truest foundation upon which all manhood is built. It is from here that moral fortitude, integrity, and character originate. Give a man strength, charisma, leadership, talent, or any other gift; but if he does not develop the Mystic in his life, all will be shallow and temporal.

To every man everywhere, God the creator is offering

life. We were designed in his image. We have been given a body for a brief time, but the part that is really us, our soul, moves onward once our heart stops beating. As a wise man so beautifully said, "You do not have a soul. You are a soul. You have a body."[2]

It is that soul that the Mystic is concerned with. For this reason, he is about anchoring a man in what is good and what is eternal. By what is good, I mean that there is absolute truth in the universe, right and wrong defined by God, not man; the Mystic orders his life under that authority. By what is eternal, I mean that there are certain things that gravity does not have any effect upon. The Mystic lives a life that is constantly seeking these things. He spends his time, talent, and money in such a way that they, along with his soul that lasts forever, are invested in things worth living and dying for.

THE MYSTIC HAS A SEMINAL CONNECTION TO GOD

A man inhabited by the Mystic is very serious about his relationship with God. The fundamental truth that God is his creator, sustainer, lover, judge, and redeemer is an obvious and inescapable reality in his life. To live only for career, money, accomplishment, and pleasure is a most childish idea for a man who embraces the Mystic. He has experienced God, not through any particular means aside from just being alive, and this awareness has permanently spoiled him from being satisfied by lower things.

We learn in the Bible that it is inexcusable to deny God's existence and presence on the earth. Creation testifies of his handiwork and reality; nothing else is needed.[3] No matter what the reason of the age tells us, the certainty of God is proven, without needing to open a Bible, to anyone who examines it through science, reason, philosophy, and moral arguments. The amount of common sense and objective proof one can find for this is inexhaustible and undeniable.

I urge the reader to, if necessary to understand the Mystic, explore these things further. Suffice to say, if we open our eyes only a little to the possibility of things beyond what we know, are told, and can touch and see, we quickly realize that men are more than random accidents living pointless lives of no consequence, future, value, or purpose. But that is another discussion.

THE MYSTIC DEPENDS ONLY AND WHOLLY UPON GOD FOR LIFE

The Mystic fears God, and rightly so. For this reason, he depends on God for everything. As previously stated, man was created by God, and thus will operate correctly if he is filled, energized, and guided by his inventor. However, in a grand act that defines the very essence of love, that inventor allowed man to choose his allegiance on his own. This makes for an interesting and marvelous thing: The one part of a man that God cannot and will not control, *a man's choice of him*, is the one thing that pleases God most.

Men can shun, grieve, deny, and quench the Spirit of God. Conversely, we can welcome, be filled with, delight, and be led by the same. If we were his idea, then we need his indwelling to properly function, and without it we will not. A well-known New Testament passage details what Paul the Apostle calls "the fruit of the Spirit."[4] Notice it is not *fruits* of the Spirit, as is often taught, but *fruit* of the Spirit, singular. That is, we are not talking here about things that we get, but *a thing* that exists rather independent of our part in it; it is the fruit of someone else's presence.

Many sit in churches and believe that if they study enough or work enough or deny sin enough that they will become a mirror of this list of nine fruits. No. These are not things we become as we "get holier." Rather, these are things that characterize God himself, and they show when he is in us. He does not make these things; he *is* these

135

things. A person who invites God into his life looks this way because God is being seen. The Mystic is wholly dependent on God in this way. He realizes that without a movement of the numinous in his life, he is all rot and death. He understands that any good that does come out of him originates from God who dwells inside of him.

MYSTICS ARE NOT PLACATED BY THE PLEASURES AND ENJOYMENTS OF EARTH

With such an appetite for that which remains forever, the Mystic is less interested in the temporary things of earth. That is not to say that earthly things are all bad; they were given to us by God for our enjoyment. However, they were meant to point us to God and cause us to hunger for him. One of the great sins of mankind - idolatry - is simply worshipping one of these pointers rather than Him to whom they are pointing. It is stopping short, making God in our image so that we do not have to live according to his rule. It is building our own kingdom rather than being subjects of his.

The Mystic is disinterested in the empires that men build. He might have been a drunkard or philanderer in the past; he might have large sums of money or the accolades of many. But he has encountered an ache in his soul when the joy of these things subsides, leaving him feeling empty. He realizes that such a void can only be filled with something beyond, and that is God. Armed with this knowledge, he makes God the primary pursuit of his life.

Smitten by the supernatural, he will only be satisfied with what it offers. David Brainerd expressed all at once a disdain for the things of earth and a voracious appetite for those of heaven. He writes, "Oh! I feel that if there is no God, though I might live forever here, and enjoy not only this, but all other worlds, I should be ten thousand times more miserable than a toad. This day I saw clearly that I should never be happy, yea, that God Himself could not make me happy, unless I could be in a capacity to 'please and glorify him forever.' Take away this, and admit me into all the fine heavens that can be conceived of by men or angels, and I should still be miserable forever."[5]

MYSTICS DO NOT COMPARTMENTALIZE GOD
Being urged on by this hunger for the supernatural, the Mystic now has an expansive buffet from which he may dine on things divine. Religious men find God when they sit in church, but less as they drive to church or eat a meal after church. The Mystic is not like these men; he is able to access the glory of God anywhere. He is like David in the Bible: "I awake and you are with me."[6] He does not need any particular place, person, type of music, or the absence of any of these to encounter God.

There are many that claim to know God just like many claim to be in love, but in both cases it is self-centered infatuation. This is a normal stage in the process of love and commitment, and it applies to both human and divine relationships. In both cases, the feelings of infatuation are really a type of lower, animal love. The lovers feel something, but it is not because they care for the other. Perhaps they do a small bit, but mostly these feelings stem from the way the other makes them feel. This type of love has no real cost and usually does not last very long.

The Mystic is beyond such base levels of affection. He does not look to his faith as some sort of stimulant or thrill ride. Rather, he sees God in everything and reacts to that presence. What were perhaps the self-gratifying origins of his faith have been worked through, and it now functions primarily apart from feeling. He realizes that God does not exist, and is not near, because man wills or believes it to be; *God simply is* whether or not a man recognizes it. More and more, this truth becomes his paradigm, and from it he is able to search for God in anything, anywhere, anytime.

MYSTICS SEARCH FOR GOD IN EVERYTHING

Perhaps this is what Jesus meant when he encouraged us to have the faith of a child. We are told that the glory of God covers all the earth. This is an invitation – not to a church building or meeting, though we may find God there – to open our senses to the sky, a cedar, a song, the human in front of us, a good cup of coffee, the scent of good pipe tobacco; and recognize the beauty of God all around us, beckoning us, inviting us, pulling us upward toward something great.

A man and his dog walking through the woods teach us much about these things. "I mean this amazing sense of feeling accompanied, of not being alone even when there's no one else around. It was as if the forest herself was Somebody and my dog and I were this Somebody's friends. It was as if everything, the whole world, was a Somebody - Somebody who loved me, Somebody who knew all my thoughts and feelings and cherished them. My dog taught me to believe in it. Her insistent, regular, faithful returning to me even while running and sniffing almost everywhere was her saying to me something like, 'Isn't this wonderful, isn't it wonderful that we're here with Somebody and Somebody loves us?' "[7]

This is far more than animism or some sort of love for "mother earth." This is two creatures sensing the presence of their Creator – Almighty God – all around them. The author, a Christian monk, is amazed by it all. Later in the same work he speaks of the wax and wane of his faith: how there are temptations to grow cold, how they are suddenly powerless in light of such moments of discovery, and how his faith is renewed. "Used to God! Good Lord, what a fool I must be!"[8]

MYSTICS KEEP LOOKING UP DESPITE THE CHANGING OF SEASONS

While the presence of God does cover the earth, there are

degrees by which we may experience what seems like more or less of him from season to season. There are many factors that affect this seeming reduction or increase in our ability to perceive and access God. These influences include our level of faith, the amount of stress in our life, the impact of others upon us, and the provident work of God in any particular season.

For a long time I have pondered these things and at some point I developed a framework to help process these changings of season in my life. The framework serves as a reference point of where one has been, providing perspective when in a season of difficulty. There are five levels, ordered from low to high experience of supernatural things: dearth, faith, shallows, ascending, and beyond.

"Dearth" is characterized by no awareness of God at all. In this season God is not apparent to us in any way. This may be as a result of sin or poor choices on our part that have removed us from the things that allow us to experience God. We might also find ourselves here because of some trial or tragedy. In any case it is not a good place to be; these are the times we feel most like throwing it all away and living as if there were no God.

"Faith" is the next level up. When we find ourselves in this place, we are required to muster memories of our past spiritual breakthroughs as equity in order to continue on. We feel very little appearance of anything supernatural in our life, but there is just enough to keep us moving with eternity in view. Often in these seasons it is others who keep our heads above water.

"Shallows" typify most of the experience of people of faith. In these times we have a general sense of the nearness of God; access to him is not difficult, and inspiration comes naturally. We are wading in shallow waters, not overwhelmed, but enough to feel that we are part of something very wonderful. Most church services and personal times of prayer and devotion fit into this category.

"Ascending" is the next category, and this is where the presence of God becomes so evident that we feel as if time were moving slowly or not at all. These seasons are more rare and might last for a few hours or a few days, maybe even weeks. In these times we feel as if our faith is impervious to any trial; we feel that nothing in life is overly bothersome or could have any real negative effect on us. These are the milestones in our faith and life that we remember very clearly many years later; they mark us and shape us. They should be cherished, for they are not dispensed very liberally.

"Beyond" is the final term I would use to describe these things. If a man finds himself in this place he is truly in a sacred moment, and should kick off his shoes, for the beyond is very rare to experience this side of heaven. It is, in fact, heaven, or a taste of it. These sort of experiences only happen a handful of times, if at all. It is here that he can be transported to other realities, visit with supernatural beings, or perhaps experience an audible or tangible visitation of God himself. We read about these meetings in the Bible, but even there they are few and far between. People still have them in modern times, and vividly remember them decades later; but these experiences are not talked about much, as they are too special to speak of.

Using this framework as a grid for evaluating our spiritual experience, we can find the Mystic in any of these five places at any time; and in all of them he is able to keep moving forward toward God. He knows that his journey of faith will look different at different seasons, and he keeps pressing on no matter how apparent or unapparent God seems to him at any given time.

THE MYSTIC IS ALWAYS RESPONSIVE TO A BURNING BUSH MOMENT

Now we have seen that the Mystic functions in a sort of paradox; it is true that the glory of God is everywhere, and it is also true that there are times that we feel nothing of it. Living in this tension, the hunger for the ascending and the beyond urges a Mystic man forward. This hunger maintains that sobriety in his spirit. He goes about his day, doing the dishes, changing the oil, driving on this or that errand. But during all of these activities he is always aware, for at any moment God might intervene.

In Exodus chapter three we have a record of one of these interventions. Moses is walking around in the wilderness, taking care of his sheep. It is a normal day - a normal, boring day most likely. Suddenly, in the midst of the rational, something transrational occurs. God appears to him as a bush that is afire but not consumed. Moses chooses to turn aside and investigate further; he does, and before long he is receiving a download from God himself, one that changes his life.[9]

A key thing to understand here: It is because Moses stopped that he moved, perhaps, from the shallows to the beyond. There was a cause and effect relationship in his paying attention and turning aside.[10] While that might seem obvious, we still might wonder why we do not experience these sort of things. Then we must ask ourselves if we are willing to turn aside when they are initiated. God is not begging followers; he presents himself to us, but we must stop what we are doing, sit down at the table, and eat. A.W. Tozer left us with a simple but haunting statement regarding this: "God waits to be wanted."[11] If we do not come to the table, the meal is missed. A man can go his entire life working a muck-rake while all the while there is a golden crown over his head, though he is unaware of it.[12]

There is an inspiring story told about John Wimber, one of the great church leaders of the modern era, that illustrates this point. Wimber had a tremendous influence on the modern worship experience as we know it, defining much of church culture as it is expressed in present times. He was among the first songwriters that introduced an accessible style of worship that broadened the expression and invitation of Christianity to include an entire new generation. His influence, and music, will impact the world for future generations.

His wife, Carol, wrote his biography, *The Way it Was*, after his death. She tells a story of what would be one of his final moments on earth. After years of suffering, criticism, betrayal, cancer, a stroke, and heart surgery, they were arriving home after a difficult stay in the hospital. She writes: "We came home on Saturday so that we wouldn't miss church on Sunday. When I had parked the car in the garage, John didn't follow me into the house. After a while I went out to see what was keeping him and found him still in the car listening to a worship tape. I bent over to look in the window and he looked up at me with a big unselfconscious smile – like a child – and said, 'Isn't it beautiful, Carol? Isn't worship beautiful?' "[13]

This man exemplified the Mystic. Caught in a moment of transcendence, he saw a burning bush moment and went with it. This characterized his entire life, and because of that his legacy has lasting and widespread impact.

THE MYSTIC LOVES TO BE ALONE
It is easier to belong to a group than to God.[14] The Mystic, smitten by the presence of God in his life, is willing to leave the crowd in order to search alone for God. He realizes that while there is great value to corporate assembly large and small, it was alone that people like Moses, Ezekiel, and Jesus himself found their rest in God. Jesus often got away by himself to a lonely place to pray; the Mystic follows this example regularly.

Leonard Ravenhill speaks fiercely to this. "The aspirant for spiritual wealth and for the ear of God will know much loneliness and will eat much of 'the bread of affliction.' He may not know too much about family or social opposition; on the other hand, he may. But this is sure, he will know much of soul conflict, and of silences (which may create misunderstandings), and of withdrawal from even the best of company. For lovers love to be alone, and the high peaks of the soul are reached in solitude."[15]

MYSTICS BRING THE BEYOND INTO THE PRESENT

A prayer you have likely heard goes like this: "Our Father in heaven, holy is your name; your kingdom come, your will be done on earth as it is in heaven."[16] Jesus prayed that prayer and in doing so taught his followers how to pray. That prayer is a dangerous one. If we pray it and have any understanding of what we are asking for, we should put on a crash helmet and strap ourselves in, for incredible things happen around those who say these words in faith.

What we are asking for when we invite the king of the universe to come among us is this: As there is no sin in heaven, eradicate sin here. As there is no illness in heaven, eliminate it here. As there is no resistance to your reign in heaven, may it be so here. This prayer, along with many other New Testament teachings, grants the followers of Jesus the authority to loose that which is then and beyond into the now and here. We have the keys to do this; we are inviting heaven to come take place on earth. We actually believe that God joins us in our church meetings, devotional times, and dinner prayers.

The Mystic sees this invitation as a way of life every day. Whether it be through a prayer, a kind act, or a simple kind word, a man possessed with Mystic faith is on a mission from God. Henri Nouwen, after a near death experience, writes about an awakening to these things. While walking along a roadside one icy day, he was struck by the protruding mirror of a passing van. This put him in the hospital for many months, during which at one point he did not anticipate continuing living.

An incredible soberness came over him as he hung

between two worlds. In these moments, his life flashed before him, and he experienced what we will call a few moments in heaven. He writes of the realization of how petty so many grudges and judgments were that existed in his heart, once they were viewed from the other side. He released all of these and felt the peace of God come over him. Upon his unexpected recovery, he had a new resolve, that he would speak and act *from the other side* while still in the present world.[17]

When I was in my late teens I discovered religion. Up to this time I had no idea who God was. We never talked about anything of this sort in my house; there was no prayer, no Bible, no church - ever. Besides that, things were rather dysfunctional, as the members of my household dabbled in illegal drug use, crime, jail time, witchcraft, voodoo, and worse. There were periods several months long when my younger brother and I lived in a house all alone and took care of ourselves, neither of us old enough to drive.

I always imagined there was a God out there somewhere. I remember when I was a little boy, up at the top of a tree I'd climbed, staring into the sky, pondering the mysteries of life. I remember sitting in school, being told I evolved from an amoeba, sure that this could not be true. The older I got the more trouble I found, and under the influence of the environment in which I grew up, by the time I was seventeen things looked pretty bleak.

One bright spot was a karate class that I drove myself to as soon as I got a license. I was there a lot, and there were a number of men who I began looking up to as father figures. One of them, an optometrist, approached me in the parking lot one night with a large book in his outstretched hand. It was a Bible. He was perceptive and had some idea of the chaos going on in my life, and encouraged me that God was seeking me, and I would find him if I were to look. I took the Bible home and began reading it intensively.

After a few months of this, I had a basic understanding on the key issues of life. God was real, and he made everything, including mankind, but we chose to reject him. I was a malefactor, living in a sin-cursed world which had invited the judgment of God upon it. God, being very loving, made an invitation of his own: Any repentant person wishing to return to him could receive forgiveness and complete absolution through the redemptive work of Jesus Christ. Those that did could then live the rest of their lives on earth with God as their king, living a life of good, undoing the darkness in the world, and looking forward to the hope of heaven.

All of this appeared very good and right to me, and at the right time - to put it plainly - God showed up in my bedroom one day while I was reading my new Bible and thought I was all alone. I believed and repented and received. He filled my heart consummately; the experience was like a bomb going off inside of me from which I have never recovered.

It was at that initial invitation for God to enter my life that my journey began into the world of the Mystic. Since then I have led, loved, fought, laughed, created, mourned, and learned better as a result of the Mystic being the foundation upon which all of these are built.

The Mystic is the part of a man that hungers for the supernatural. He has experienced God and lives a life according to higher principles as a result. He seeks the best for those around him, inhabited by and reflecting the goodness, mercy, and peace of God above.

But the Mystic is not always welcome. For the man who rejects his origin and sustenance as coming from God, the Degenerate takes control, steering a course toward ruin. In contrast, the man who dabbles in man-made religion for his own amusement plays the game of the Hypocrite.

THE DEGENERATE

The work of the Degenerate across the globe is pervasive. The effects of his influence are easy to spot; where there is murder, hatred, brutality, destruction, genocide, slavery, and injustice, he is close by. He functions out of a godless paradigm. Having no belief in God, he has no moral absolutes, nor does he believe there is any consequence to his actions. Therefore, anything goes, and man left to himself as such finds himself in a dark place.

The title of Degenerate has deep meaning, for this man has experienced a type of reverse evolution. He has left his original state, one that was glorious because he was made in the image of glory, and since deteriorated into a much different condition. He is decaying, both in body and spirit. The fruit of his life is not life but instead the things that accompany death.

Degenerates shake their fist at God in rebellion against his claim on their life. In some cases, the Degenerate man does believe in God, but has become bitter because of life's difficulties. In others, he loves pleasure and debasement; and knowing that those things and God cannot coexist, he protests against a God who would rein him in and object to his self-destruction. The Degenerate can spiral to a place where he wants to destroy others and himself.

We could look at the product of a man's life in this state and see things that may appear shiny on the outside but have no life within. A man might have some balance in his life, exhibiting the qualities of a King, Jester, or Artist.

He might have amassed millions of dollars and have buildings named after him. But if he is a Degenerate, none of these things will have any value beyond what is seen. None of it will survive the trip to heaven, nor be remembered in the afterlife.

It might seem that a man in this rut would have the conviction or common sense to change his ways before it is too late. But that would be underestimating the depravity in man and deny his desperate need for the Mystic. Part of the process of the Degenerate's degradation is that after a short time in his journey, his conscience becomes crusted over and numb. It is at this point that he can no longer feel; the fact is that he can no longer feel good nor evil.

For this reason he becomes less and less likely to turn back toward God, and more absorbed in and addicted to evil. We see this progression in men as they start small with some playful addiction, and before long have lost everything because that addiction has grown into a monster and taken over. What started very small quickly got out of hand. In some cases, a man can go so far down the path of the Degenerate that he cannot even be reached by God.[18]

This is the fate of a man that denies the Mystic and instead chooses the path of the Degenerate. But there is another dangerous criminal to this archetype who even appears quite pious on the outside. The truth is, his faith is as nominal as they come, a scam as equally reprehensible as the one being played by the Degenerate. This great religious pretender goes by the name of Hypocrite.

THE HYPOCRITE
Our final imposter is among the most dangerous because he is so deceptive. A man can think himself a Mystic while in reality he is a Hypocrite. In a sense, all of us are hypocrites, but some go far enough to take the title because it is their way of life.

147

The Hypocrite is characterized by a pretend, fake, lukewarm faith. Hypocrites often appear very slick on the outside, and they are welcomed by others of their same nature. Sometimes churches or entire religious groups consist of a large number of these charlatans, patting one another as they march along in a self-righteous parade.

The Hypocrite values religion, but only in that it can advance him in the opinions of others and in his own eyes. He does not really want to take part in any serious surrender of his inner life. Rather, he dabbles in righteousness in order to appease the moral calling upon him; but it is less of a pursuit and more of a proprietary obligation. He is very happy to return home after some religious meeting, put his Hypocrite clothes in the closet, and return to his secret life of compromise.

Like the Degenerate, the Hypocrite's name has meaning. It is derived from the Greek word *hypokrites,* which itself is a compound word, made up of two words that mean "under" and "play." This word found a good bit of use in the historic Greek context, as theater actors wore large masks as part of their character costume. Their job was to play the character from under the mask, hence the title *hypokrite.* In short, they were pretenders. Of course, these days the title has come to mean a person who is pretending to be something they are not, and that is exactly the case for our discussion.

The Hypocrite might live a long life of playacting, but like the Degenerate, judgment on his pretentious ways is swift and horrifying. The exposure of hypocrisy is a violent business; in some cases such men are chased from their stages with a scourge of cords. The true Mystic passionately hates hypocrisy and will expose it, starting with that which he sees in his own self.

Bunyan's Christian is somewhat deceived by a collection of expert Hypocrites, but is relieved by the good Evangelist, a master Mystic who will not stand for these fakes: "This Legality is not able to set you free from thy burden. Mr. Worldly Wiseman is an alien, and Mr. Legality is a cheat; and as for his son Civility, notwithstanding his simpering looks, he is but a hypocrite, and cannot help thee. There is nothing in all this noise that thou hast heard of these sottish men, but a design to beguile thee of thy salvation."[19]

THE DECISION TO ASCEND LIKE A MYSTIC
We have come to decision number eight; will a man...

- demoralize like a Degenerate,
- pretend like a Hypocrite,
- or, like a Mystic, *devote oneself to God and experience the things beyond?*

In making this decision, a man must ask himself a few difficult questions:

- Without thinking too deeply, right in this moment, which of these three do I most identify with?
- If asked, how would the people who are closest to me describe me in this regard?

HOMEWORK
Before moving on, take some time (one day or perhaps one week) to ponder the things you have read about the Mystic and his imposters. Consider these questions as you interact with this material:

1. In the arenas below, are you a Degenerate, a Hypocrite, or a Mystic?
   a. Work
   b. Marriage, if married; or if not, in a pre-marriage relationship
   c. With my children, if I have any
   d. With my extended family, in-laws, and/or grandchildren
   e. Friendships
   f. Social groups (neighborhood, clubs) and religious groups (church)

2.   As you grow in self-awareness, wonder…
   a. Why am I the way I am?
   b. Who and what has positively influenced the Mystic in me?
   c. What has led to the takeover of the Degenerate or the Hypocrite in me?
   d. What past or current life events and memories come to mind as I ask myself these questions?

3.   As you think of the future, ponder…
   a. What things do I do on a daily basis in order to connect with God?
   b. In what ways is my relationship with God pouring out onto others?
   c. What might I remove from my life that would grow the Mystic in me?
   d. What specific behaviors might I start practicing or rekindle to this end?

Final Thoughts

"I am far less amazing than I ever thought, and far more." [1]

As we have seen, there are many different facets of manhood. All of these, when embraced to the fullest, come together to make a man the best he can be:

A pioneering King,
a caring Lover,
a vigorous Fighter,
a playful Jester,
a creative Artist,
a solemn Mourner,
a teachable Wizard,
and a spiritual Mystic.

It is interesting to consider how each of these

expressions of manhood can influence the others. For example, a man who embraces the Wizard will do himself much good as he grows in being a King, for they complement one another quite nicely. Similarly, the Jester is necessary for the Mourner, for laughter is good medicine for a sad heart. Fighter energy fueling a Mystic can spark reform in an entire nation. There are many possibilities.

The same is true in the negative sense. A King who has no need for the Artist will soon stop leading as he chases either the spirit of the age (the Copycat) or his own unrealistic whims and vain imaginations (the Dreamer). Dreamer Kings do not reign for very long. Another example: The care expressed by a Lover who abandons the Jester will soon dry up (the Prude) or deteriorate into decadence (the Fool). Prudish Lovers become Loners and foolish ones become Hedonists.

There are such detours for each of these expressions of manhood, and as they have a systemic relationship with one another, the corruption of one can quickly contribute to the polluting of the others. However, the opposite is also true, and with tempering and balance a man will keep the course and stay true to who he was meant to be. In this sense, health begets health. The synergy of all eight archetypes pulsing within a man will cause him to grow in character and depth.

In this final chapter we will discuss that growth process. While we have examined eight decisions that define us, the truth is that becoming a healthy, well-balanced man requires much more than just making a one-time decision. We need a long-term strategy for health; one that may take years of dedicated effort to bear fruit in our lives. In order to achieve continual growth in all areas of life, we must establish practices that push us along the way, and we must consistently follow them. The rest of this chapter will outline five practices that are critical to achieving balance. They are as follows:

1. Figure out who you are
2. Play your strengths and attend to your weaknesses
3. Seek out mentors
4. Give yourself an hour of every day of your life
5. Pace yourself by embracing slowness

PRACTICE #1: FIGURE OUT WHO YOU ARE

For a moment we must now suspend all thinking about the eight archetypes and consider what makes us tick from another perspective. The question is this: *Who are you really?* Self-awareness is an uncommon thing these days. The man is rare who is brave enough to bring to mind his past history and experiences and then wonder in what ways they have contributed to who he is today.

The "who you really are" is influenced by three things:

A. Nature – who you are destined to be. This is the predetermination made by your DNA and the destiny that God ordained for you before you even existed.

B. Nurture – who you were shaped into. Both positive and negative life experiences contribute to this formation that primarily occurred in our childhood but extends into adulthood.

C. Choices – who you choose to be. Irrespective of nature and nurture, the choices we make, whether good or bad, can clear a divergent path in our lives despite the two other influences.

Considering these three influences, take a minute to think about your own life.

In terms of *nature*, the truth is that one man is simply stronger than another, while another man is smarter than both. One will have an amazing voice while another cannot carry a tune. Some are naturally charismatic and able to enjoy large crowds, while others crave solitude.

Concerning *nurture*, there are so many influences that affect us – where we were born, our economic status, the values of our parents, our access to health care and education, and the presence of positive role models in our life – just to name a few. One person might have a big head start on another in their development in any particular area of life because of different circumstances.

As to *choices*, this is the wild card that can offset the positive or negative effects of the two above. A person with low natural aptitude and horrible life circumstances can make a succession of good choices and go far. Conversely, a person born with all the goods and into an environment of opportunity can end up living in a gutter if they mix with the wrong crowd or do not take advantage of the prospects presented to them.

Despite our respective situations, suffice to say we are where we are because of these three influencing factors. Now, with that in mind, in order to find out who we truly are, we must probe deeper. Whether a man is emotionally healthy or not depends largely on which "self" he has embraced: the *false self* or the *authentic self*. These are very different.

In her fantastic work *Strengthening the Soul of Your Leadership*, Ruth Haley Barton explains the differences between the two. The *authentic self* "encompasses everything that makes us who we are: our genetics, innate orientations and capacities, our personality, heredity and life-shaping experiences, and the time and place into which we were born."[2] This is the pure, unadulterated, original design of who we were meant to be, at our best, in the mind of God our creator.

But there is an imposter: the *false self*. Life brings difficulty and pressure, and under the weight of these we are likely to abandon the true self and become someone else, just as in a storm we lose our bearings and perhaps become lost. "By the time we even know that there is such a thing as a true or authentic self, the false self has already taken over to the extent that it is hard to tell what is false and what is true. But if we are willing to pay attention, we can catch glimpses of the true self by noticing what brings deep gladness and a sense of meaning to our existence. Some of the best hints about who we really are come from memories of unguarded moments in childhood and youth, moments when we were caught up in the essence of being rather than driven by self-conscious doing and performing. This essential self existed before we had anything to prove, before we had any sense of what was socially acceptable or useful, before we needed to figure out how to make a living."[3]

When grown-up life happens to us, as referred to earlier in the chapter on the Jester, it is very easy to see how we develop coping mechanisms and adaptive behaviors in order to survive. But, to our detriment, sometimes these behaviors are not healthy ones; in the process of managing life, it is very easy to leave the essential self behind and allow the false self to take over.

In order to recover the essential self, we must find out who that is. As we just learned, there are certain defining things and experiences that are core to who we are; these were already forming in us while we were very young. Whether they have been allowed to bloom or were crushed, they are valid and essential to what brings us a sense of meaning. In order to find out who we are, we must consider what those defining things are in our lives.

Here is a very simple exercise that will guide you in doing that:

1.   Think of your younger years, from the time you
      first remember anything until adulthood (age 18).
      Think of experiences that you remember very
      clearly, ones that brought you deep joy and
      meaning. Don't think too hard – whatever the
      first ten memories are that come to mind, jot
      these down quickly below under MEMORY. We
      will trust that your subconscious mind will bring
      out the proper and defining things.

For example, you might remember a moment on a
playground where you saw someone being bullied and felt a
sense of anger at this injustice. Or you might have a vivid
memory of the joy of playing a harmonica all alone in your
bedroom at an early age, picking out and inventing melodies
to pass time - you might even remember the melodies your
younger self breathed into life.

MEMORY   CORE/ESSENCE
i.   _____
ii.   _____
iii.   _____
iv.   _____
v.   _____
vi.   _____
vii.   _____
viii.   _____
ix.   _____
x.   _____

2.   Now consider each of these ten memories more
      closely. For each, discover what the core of that
      experience was all about. This will be a single

word or short phrase that captures the essence of the moment and reveals something about you. Jot this down under CORE/ESSENCE.

To our examples again. The moment on the playground could be designated as "a sense of justice for the weak." The moment with the harmonica might be labeled as "a desire and joy to create music." And so on. These answers tell you what your essential self looks like.

3.   Lastly it is time for a reckoning. For each of the ten things that you have listed in part two, ask yourself this question: *Am I still doing or expressing this in my life in some way today?* The answer to this question reveals whether or not you are expressing your essential self. If not, the sad truth is that it has been lost and left behind as you moved on to what you considered the more important things of adulthood.

This is not to say that a man should not find employment and earn money and take care of things; in the midst of our dreams and aspirations, life must go on. The point here is to discover if - as we pursue our work and paying of bills and maintaining relationships and growing up - you and I are still able to be the person we really are and do the things we were meant to do. The answer to this question could be encouraging, or very discouraging.

If this exercise has brought you a sense of affirmation, hats off to you for keeping your essential self alive. On the contrary, if many or most of the memories have not resurfaced nor borne any fruit in your life, and you feel that you are living behind a false self, there is hope. The next step is to examine why you detoured from your essential self and how you can recover who you are meant to be. The remaining practices will help you in that process.

PRACTICE #2: PLAY YOUR STRENGTHS AND ATTEND TO YOUR WEAKNESSES

At the beginning of this study it was noted that of the eight archetypes, you or I might naturally emphasize a few of these persons more strongly than others. We were each created uniquely, and while we may seek health and balance in all eight of the personalities mentioned, we will express certain ones more naturally than the rest. The vital thing to our health as men is that we have a correct expression of all eight, even those that have a smaller role in our lives.

Once we come to terms with who we are, we are able to determine which of these eight roles we more naturally express, and can then play those strengths. The athlete that secures a football scholarship does not do so because of his ability in trigonometry; while he may be an excellent mathematician, it is his ability to run, tackle, pass, catch, or kick that secures his future. A person applying for employment at an investment firm would do well to attend his interview prepared to discuss his experience with stocks and bonds rather than his achievements in the middle school beta club. Each man is different. Each of us has natural ability and gifting in certain areas, and in order to be who we were created to be, we must focus our energy and play our strengths.

At the same time, it is important to pay attention to our weaknesses. We might naturally express one personality while giving little attention to another because we feel it is not needed. While it might not seem important, giving attention to the areas where we have lower aptitude can make us more well-rounded and increase our influence.

For example, consider the Hollywood action star Dolph Lundgren. While he is primarily known as an actor with a stunning physique and intimidating presence, beneath the surface is a man who has done chemistry on a graduate-school level and supported efforts to end human trafficking through movie production and non-profit organizations.[4] The Fighter is complimented by the Wizard and the Lover.

All this is to say that we do well to play our strengths and bolster our weaknesses. Think again for a moment about the eight archetypes: King, Lover, Fighter, Jester, Artist, Mourner, Wizard, and Mystic. You might consult the "At a Glance" appendix to refresh yourself with the purpose, decision, and qualities of each. Next, use the space below to designate which three you feel are your HIGHEST NATURAL APTITUDE and then which three you feel are your LOWEST NATURAL APTITUDE. Write the two that remain in the MIDDLE:

HIGHEST NATURAL APTITUDE

1. _____
2. _____
3. _____

MIDDLE

4. _____
5. _____

LOWEST NATURAL APTITUDE

6. _____
7. _____
8. _____

Now, consider your three areas of strength and ponder:

- Are these archetypes playing a part in my hobbies? At the job I am working?

Now, consider your three areas of weakness and answer:

- How can I give attention to these archetypes in order that I may grow their influence in my life?
- What areas of my life would benefit most if I were to grow in these weaknesses?

PRACTICE #3: SEEK OUT MENTORS

Call them teachers, coaches, trainers, or something else – the people in our lives who fill these roles can make a dramatic difference in us. It is mentors who teach us to read and write and do arithmetic. The same help us learn to drive and write a resumé. Mentors apprentice us. Whether it be in the skill of carpentry or surgery, before you become a master you must first walk in the shoes of journeyman or resident. Mentors also guide us through premarital counseling, conduct us in an orchestra, and train us to endure a triathlon.

Considering the importance of the mentor/mentee relationship, it is a sad truth that most men are lost in a sea of questions and struggles without anyone to guide them. The heavy emphasis on mentorship in our time and culture gives great attention to external issues, but little weight to internal matters. A man may get training to advance his career, but not to enrich his marriage; a man may be coached to work in tandem with a rowing team, but be taught very little about financial responsibility and avoiding debt. There is so little value, even among most people of faith, on any true sense of man-to-man mentoring. The reason for this is that most men do not want to be transparent.

Becoming transparent requires humility and invites accountability; but there is a price to pay in order to acquire both of these. Talking openly about the real issues that men face is a scary thing. Most men's gatherings, even among churchmen, consist of activity and talk centered on sports, current events, pop culture, or other shallow topics – anything to avoid what the men in the room are really dealing with. Were you or I to sit with a group of men and talk candidly about our addiction to money, or our compulsive eating habits, or our struggle for sexual purity, the room might go silent. It's much easier to talk about who won the game.

In the face of such posing and overcompensation so prevalent in our culture is the man who will seek out mentors for himself. This practice, though rare in our times, was actually quite common not so long ago, and still is in many parts of the world.

Robert Hicks tells of his experience observing Middle-Eastern Bedouin tribes on the edge of the Sinai. Stopping in the evening for a rest, passing caravans would set up camp in the desert. A fire, roasted meat, the breaking of bread, and hours of conversation were next. Young and old reclined on blankets and pillows, sipping hot tea, reviewing the matters of the day. "The most common feature I noticed from my vantage point was the white-robed, gray-haired, bearded men gathered in circles, drinking their tea, and speaking with great intensity as illustrated by their hand gestures. These were elders, doing what elders do."[5]

The man who wishes to expand his soul will create these pit-stop experiences and fill his life with mentors. Now, of course, we are talking about soul growth. The topics discussed in these relationships are less news and politics, and more integrity and character. In these mentoring experiences we discuss our ambition, our relational conflict, our griefs, our sins, our failures, our great challenges; the things that keep us up late and wake us up early. We proactively seek out men from whom we can learn and make good use of our time with them, baring our soul and learning what we can.

A meeting with such a mentor is a sacred thing and has some of that old-world feel to it. It's more than an hour appointment that starts and ends abruptly. We let our guard down and become honest about our struggles and questions. I've even found that including a campfire and a pipe, filled with my favorite fresh tobacco, goes far to create a natural and relational atmosphere in which soul mentoring can occur. Mentoring can be done on a long walk or a hike in the cold. Whatever the context, it feels less like an obligatory meeting and more like a convergence of two souls.

Practically, I suggest informal monthly appointments. Search for someone you look up to – a man who, perhaps, strongly evidences one or more of the archetypes we've discussed in this book. Find someone with some wrinkles and scars. Referencing the second practice above, perhaps one of your areas of low aptitude can be built up by finding a man who seems to be strong in that way. These monthly meetings should be scheduled, e.g. the first Saturday of each month at 7am. Invite a potential mentor out for coffee or breakfast, pay the tab, and ask questions. Be brave – you can waste a good morning talking about nothing, or you can get real and bring up your deep questions. Doing so gives the mentor permission to be real himself and speak into your life, and that's when soul growth really happens.

This sort of informal mentoring relationship might last a few months or many years. Mentors will come in and out of your life – there are different seasons for different relationships. At times, I have had four different monthly meetings such as we are discussing; at other times, only one. The goal is to proactively surround yourself with men from whom you can learn; and it cannot be underscored enough – *you* must make this happen. If you do not, chances are it will not happen. When men are younger, they commonly believe that sages will seek them out and teach them everything they know, perhaps filling the role that their own father left vacant. This is rarely the case, and as much as a man might talk about wanting elders and coaches in his life, it is the one who initiates these types of relationships that receives the benefits of them.

There is a time and place for paid counseling, and this sort of objective relationship is necessary in certain circumstances. But it is often the informal (and relatively free) mentoring that has an equal or greater influence on our lives. Put just fifty people in a room and, if we are willing to expel the Mannequin in each of us, what is left is a raw bundle of collective energy and experience that holds a tremendous amount of power.

It is sad that this does not happen in much of first world church culture. Why pay good money for an hour of counseling when, within a few feet on a Sunday morning, there are people that have walked before us? The motley crew of scarred survivors are all there: widows and widowers, recovering drug addicts, parents bereaved of their children, cancer survivors, combat veterans, blended families, survivors of sexual abuse, and many more. The scars tell stories and they should be shared. A college degree or office chair is not needed for counseling and mentorship – rather, only two people and a small dose of humility.

In closing, take a moment to think of past and current mentors in your life. List them below.

PAST AND CURRENT MENTORS
1. _____
2. _____
3. _____

Now, consider potential future mentors. List them below.

POTENTIAL FUTURE MENTORS
1. _____
2. _____
3. _____

Choose one of these with whom you have not made any connection on a deep level. Resolve that by the end of the week, you will have contacted this man and made arrangements for a good, old-fashioned, Bedouin-style fireside discussion.

PRACTICE #4: GIVE YOURSELF AN HOUR OF EVERY DAY OF YOUR LIFE

Many years ago, during the last semester of my senior year of college, I made a decision that has had a dramatic effect on my life ever since. Up until that point, mornings were a mad rush – too little sleep, combined with youthful disorganization and procrastination, had me always hurrying and rarely at rest. When my degree was nearly complete, things were slowing down a bit, and for whatever reason I began the practice of waking an hour early to pray, read, think, and compose myself for the day.

In order to save money, I was renting a bedroom from a family near the university I attended. I remember the creaky trundle bed, the décor of the bedroom, and the little black and white cat (his name was Hercules) that would bite and bat at my bookmark as I attempted these daily quiet times. I also remember something shifting in my soul at that time before I entered the mad world of full-on life after college graduation. It was the decision to create a daily space where I could face myself before I ran off to face everybody else (and they, in turn, would face me). It became, and has been now for decades, the single most life-giving practice I have integrated into my growth as a man.

It is in these times that we find ourselves. Separating from our daily rush and focusing on simply *being* for an hour creates a composure within us from which we can go about our day and interactions with courage and integrity. In these alone times we stop and evaluate. We read and are challenged. Nothing and nobody else is around to define us, and in this space we sink our roots deep and are nourished. Blaise Pascal is known for saying, "All men's miseries derive from not being able to sit in a quiet room alone."[6] A man who sits alone and faces himself is taking a proactive and preemptive strike against those miseries.

Whether it be early morning or late at night, giving oneself an hour each day creates a time to center and re-center. Your schedule may not allow this to happen in the morning, but suffice to say this sacred daily time serves us best when it occurs before we go about our day. If we wait until the day is nearly done, busyness and exhaustion may interfere or prevent anything productive from happening. Therefore, it is best to take control of our schedule before it takes control of us. If you find yourself in the early stages of your manhood, perhaps raising a family or having small children that wander the dark halls looking for their daddy, this will prove more difficult. But the man that prioritizes his own soul health will find a way to make it happen, even if it means losing sleep.

By proactively reserving this daily time for himself, a man is making the decision that soul care is more important than productivity or the needs of others. Like we hear each time we prepare for flight on an airplane, in the event that oxygen masks appear, we must first ensure that we are breathing before we help the person next to us. Robert Bly, using the garden as an analogy of a place where inner transformation occurs, says it poignantly: "Some men entering the garden begin by getting up at 5 A.M. and keeping an hour for themselves each morning before work. A father, in order to do that, may have to resist his own insistence that his life belongs to his work, his children, and his marriage."[7]

There are a variety of things that might happen in these alone times. We might sit with the sunrise and remind ourselves of what we have planned for the day. Reading, particularly the Bible, is important; I have made the practice of reading one chapter of the Bible every day, in order. Doing this will get you through the entire thing in about three years and four months, and then you can start over. Prayer and meditation are possible, as is journaling, which in simpler terms is meditation put to paper. We need to *think* – think about what we have read, what it means for us, what God might be saying to us. Quiet time in the dark invites this sort of thinking, and it often produces insight and revelation.

Other options include fasting, writing, singing, and whatever else allows us to focus and center ourselves. One might even develop his own personal liturgy – an hour of ordered practices that come together to feed the soul. Perhaps start with a few quiet moments, listening to the world and thinking about the day. From there comes Scripture reading, meditation, writing, and a time of thanksgiving. Then study ten pages or so of whatever book you are working through. End the time with a review of your schedule, resolutions for the day, and prayer to seek the will of God in all that is ahead. Get up, head to work, and function out of a place of serenity and preparedness, a quietness from which you can face the world with courage and focus.

Very important to all of this is that we make these times enjoyable. Religious drudgery is a soul-killer, so avoid it. The expectations we put on ourselves to have an epiphany every time must be abandoned. The goal here is not to find the holy grail; rather, it is to find a thousand pieces of the holy grail, through a thousand mini-quests, over a thousand mornings in which we purpose to discover it. Nothing magical might happen, but the journey is the important part. So make it fun – brew your favorite coffee, sit in your favorite chair, perhaps by a window. Light a candle and enjoy the sensory experience. If things get boring, switch them up. Find ways to make this hour meaningful.

One more thing must be mentioned. We must not use these alone hours for merely reading the news or checking e-mail and social media updates. The hour is wasted if we are simply getting busy before we get busy. Rather, it must involve some sort of soul component as described above. It is that which invites character growth, and it must be prioritized.

PRACTICE #5: PACE YOURSELF BY EMBRACING SLOWNESS

We have come to the final pages of this book, and here I would leave you with a final practice, one that I have found to be life-changing in regard to my development as a man. Just two words: slow down.

In my youth everything seemed fast, and I moved at a quick pace to keep up. I ran fast, a five minute mile; I drove fast, sometimes in the triple digits. I worked quickly, accomplishing as much as three or four other people; observers often commented on how fast I did everything. But in my thirties, a number of things happened that worked together to force me to slow down, and while the change was difficult, I am much better for it.

A number of tragedies and events converged upon me in that season; several I have mentioned in earlier chapters, including the tragic death of my father and my daughter's years in the hospital. In this same time frame, I was working far too many hours trying to take care of a new and growing church and a new and growing family. It seemed there was never enough time in the day to slow down and enjoy life. I remember one pivotal moment when one of my sons approached me as I was typing away at my computer, working on something important. He was about seven at the time; he stood next to me, put his hand on my forearm, and said "Dad, can you...." but then stopped himself and finished the sentence with "...never mind, you're too busy." He then walked away.

This moment was a gut punch for me. Combined with the sobriety I experienced when my dad died and my daughter was born, it worked to turn me into a very different person. I realized that my life was too full, that my family needed me now more than ever, and that I needed to find myself more than ever. A counselor advised me to cut my work hours back from fifty-five to forty a week, and I did so immediately. I resigned from a regional leadership position in my denomination that took me away from home regularly for conferences and speaking engagements. I even sold my car, a high-tech turbocharged beast, and bought an old Honda Civic beater for two thousand dollars.

Life slowed down tremendously. I puttered around town in that little car - me who never got passed in my younger days, now being passed by everyone, even the grandmas. It was exhilarating to not be able to go fast and therefore not be in a rush. The limitations that life placed on me were doing wonders; I learned to eliminate hurry from my life and pace myself for the long road.

The journey is a very long one. Men need far-sightedness in order to make it more than just a few years. We must slow down so that we have margin in our lives, margin from which we can function at our best rather than always living on our leftovers or reserves. To this end, I leave you with a nugget of wisdom that comes from Herman Melville's famous book *Moby Dick*. Hidden in the story of a man's maniacal pursuit for revenge are many lessons on life. One of them speaks of the measured pace from which a man can be prepared for whatever adventure life brings him: "For the greatest accuracy at the dart, the harpooners of this world must start to their feet out of idleness, and not out of toil."[8]

As we pursue the long and difficult journey of manhood, may we slow down to a pace that allows us to enjoy the journey. May we learn from trusted mentors along the way and spend much time alone in the cultivating of our souls. May we find out who we are and what we are to be about. The rewards will be great, and as we emerge from the hard-fought battles behind and before us, we will discover more and more what it means to be a King, a Lover, a Fighter, a

Jester, an Artist, a Mourner, a Wizard, and a Mystic. In doing so, we will bless those around us, and we will grow into all that God has for us.

To that end, may you be filled with strength and courage as you continually embrace these eight decisions every man should make.

APPENDIX 1: NOTES

Author's note: The NAS Bible was used for all biblical quotes. However, in some cases it was slightly paraphrased by myself to better express the Hebrew or Greek text.

ACKNOWLEDGEMENTS
1. *The New American Standard (NAS) Bible*, Proverbs 18:24. Chicago: Moody Press, 1978. Print.

CHAPTER 1: THE KING
1. C.S. Lewis, *The Chronicles of Narnia: The Horse and His Boy* (Great Britain: HarperCollins, 1998), 310.
2. Robert Bly, *Iron John* (Boston, MA: Da Capo Press, 2015), 116.
3. *Mad Max: Fury Road*. Directed by George Miller. Hollywood: Warner Brothers, 2015.
4. The NAS Bible, John 2:25.
5. Bly, 117.

CHAPTER 2: THE LOVER
1. David Brainerd, *The Life and Diary of David Brainerd* (Peabody, MA: Hendrickson, 2006), 107.
2. The NAS Bible, Matthew 22:37-40, 1 John 1:20.
3. Ibid, The Song of Solomon 4:16.
4. St. Augustine, *Confessions* (London: J. M. Dent & Sons, 1907), 183.
5. C. S. Lewis, *The Four Loves* (New York, NY: Harcourt, Brace, 1960), 70, 89.
6. The NAS Bible, Job 33:6-7.
7. One of our textbooks for the course mentioned was *Out of the Shadows* by Patrick J. Carnes. I highly recommend this book for further understanding on the psychology of sexual addiction.

CHAPTER 3: THE FIGHTER

1. Petty, Tom. *Full Moon Fever*. MCA Records MCAD-6253, 1989, compact disc.
2. *The NAS Bible*, 1 Samuel 17.
3. Ibid, 1 Chronicles 12:8,14-15.
4. *Drive*. Directed by Nicolas Winding Refn. Los Angeles: Bold Films, 2011.
5. *The NAS Bible*, Proverbs 17:27, 29:11, 25:28.
6. Robert Hicks, *The Masculine Journey* (Colorado Springs, CO: Navpress, 1993), 128.
7. Ibid, 146.
8. Ibid, 133.
9. Bly, 160.
10. Frick, D. (2014). Introduction. *Rolling Stone Special Collector's Edition Tom Petty*, 7.

CHAPTER 4: THE JESTER

1. William A Barry Sj, Robert J Doherty, *Contemplatives in Action: The Jesuit Way* (Mahwah, NJ: Paulist Press, 2002), 78.
2. *The NAS Bible*, Ecclesiastes 7:21.
3. Ibid, Deuteronomy 12:7.
4. It is Roald Dahl who is known for saying this; I do not know where this quote originated but found it written in my journal many years ago and have remembered it since. Online research shows it coming from his book *Charlie & the Chocolate Factory*, but I am unable to provide any information beyond that for this reference.
5. Complex. "Spider-man to Spawn, How Todd McFarlane Became the Biggest Comic Book Artist Ever | Blueprint." Online video clip. YouTube. YouTube, 24 July 2017. 6 October 2017.
6. C.S. Lewis, *The Screwtape Letters* (New York, NY: HarperCollins, 2001), 66.

7. Lewis, *The Four Loves*, 135.

8. Vettriano, Jack. *The Singing Butler*. 1992. Aberdeen Art Gallery, Scotland.

CHAPTER 5: THE ARTIST

1. Cynthia Rylant, *Mr. Putter and Tabby Pour the Tea* (Orlando, FL: Harcourt Brace & Company, 1994), chapter 3, first page (no page numbers designated).

2. *The NAS Bible*, Genesis 1:1.

3. Boston. Third Stage. MCA Records MCAD-6188, 1986, compact disc.

4. *The Secret Life of Walter Mitty*. Directed by Ben Stiller. Culver City: Samuel Goldwyn Films, 2013.

5. Morgan James. "Morgan James – HUNTER Episode 5: Soul Music." Online video clip. YouTube. YouTube, 29 January 2015. 19 December 2016.

6. Jon Foreman said this. I copied these words into my journal many years ago but did not cite the source where I originally found them. It was an older interview, as I recall, featured in *Paste* magazine, but beyond that I cannot provide any details.

CHAPTER 6: THE MOURNER

1. Mallonee, Bill. V.O.L. Warner Resound 9 46309-2, 1996, compact disc.

2. Brainerd, 145.

3. John Bunyan, *The Pilgrim's Progress* (Grand Rapids, MI: Fleming H. Revell, publication date unknown, original definitive 2nd edition published 1686), 246.

4. Samuel Rutherford, *Letters of Samuel Rutherford* (Peoria, IL: Versa, 1973), 52-53.

5. Gene Edwards, *A Tale of Three Kings* (Wheaton,

IL: Tyndale, 1992), 12.

6. Miller, Jeff. This song is titled *Suffering* and is unpublished.

7. *The NAS Bible*, Ecclesiastes 10:7; Psalm 73:3-5.

8. *The NAS Bible*, Matthew 11:6.

9. *The NAS Bible*, Judges 20. This is one of those passages in the Scripture that I read a dozen times but never really processed until more recent years.

10. Nicholas Wolterstorff, *Lament for a Son* (Grand Rapids: Eerdmans, 1987), 81.

11. *The NAS Bible*, Hebrews 12:2.

12. Bunyan, 174.

13. Augustine, 155.

14. Bly, 70.

CHAPTER 7: THE WIZARD

1. St. Augustine, *Confessions*, page unknown. I am sure this quote came from this book, for I copied it into my journal years ago. But once again, I did not cite the page number.

2. *The NAS Bible*, Ecclesiastes 4:13.

3. *The NAS Bible*, Proverbs 1:5, 8:33, 10:8, 12:15, 15:5, 19:20.

4. Lewis, *The Four Loves*, p. 127.

5. *The NAS Bible*, Psalm 12:6.

6. This saying and many others like it are famously attributed to Miles Davis, but the sources are never cited.

7. Barry and Doherty, 48. Study of the Jesuit movement reveals that its quality diminished in a proportional measure to its increase in size. Sadly after the death of Ignatius, the founder of the Jesuits, this became a notable problem.

8. *The NAS Bible*, Proverbs 17:10, 27:22, 26:11.

9. *Good Will Hunting*. Directed by Gus Van Sant. Los Angeles: Miramax, 1997.

CHAPTER 8: THE MYSTIC

1. St. Ignatius, *Reminisces* (London: Penguin Books, 1996), 3.
2. This quote is often attributed to both George MacDonald and C.S. Lewis, but the source is unidentifiable.
3. *The NAS Bible*, Romans 1:20.
4. *The NAS Bible*, Galatians 5:22-23.
5. Brainerd, 68, 244.
6. *The NAS Bible*, Psalm 3:5.
7. Jeremy Driscoll, *A Monk's Alphabet* (London: Darton, Longman and Todd, 2006), 71.
8. Ibid, 126.
9. *The NAS Bible*, Exodus chapter 3.
10. Ruth Haley Barton, *Strengthening the Soul of Your Leadership* (Downer's Grove, IL: InterVarsity, 2008), 61.
11. A. W. Tozer, The Pursuit of God (Camp Hill: Christian Publications, Inc., 1993), 17.
12. John Bunyan, *The Pilgrim's Progress* (Grand Rapids: Spire books, no date listed), 192.
13. Carol Wimber, *The Way It Was* (London: Hodder & Stoughton, 1999), 202.
14. Barton, 164.
15. Revivalist Leonard Ravenhill said this, and I wrote it in my Bible over twenty years ago, but the source of this citation is unknown.
16. *The NAS Bible*, Matthew 6:9-13.
17. Henri Nouwen, *Beyond the Mirror* (New York, NY: Crossroad, 2001), 70.
18. *The NAS Bible*, see the passage in Exodus chapter 8, along with the surrounding chapters. It appears that for the first few plagues Pharaoh hardens his own heart, but by the end of the ten plagues it is God hardening his heart.
19. Bunyan, 16.

CHAPTER 9: FINAL THOUGHTS

1. This truth of this statement occurred to me and ended up in my journaling many years ago. It expresses the utter defeat and amazing freedom that we often feel all at once in our journey of faith.

2. Barton, p. 77. I am indebted to this book for providing the groundwork for this exercise.

3. Ibid, p. 78.

4. TedX Talks. "Dolph Lundgren | On healing and forgiveness | TEDxFulbrightSantaMonica." Online video clip. YouTube. YouTube, 28 October 2015. 1 November 2017.

5. Hicks, 150.

6. This quote is attributed to Blaise Pascal, found is his work *Pensées*. The page number for this citation is uncertain.

7. Bly, 142-3.

8. Peterson, Eugene. "The Unbusy Pastor." *Christianity Today*, archive from 1981, https//christianitytoday.com/pastors/1981/summer/eugene-peterson-unbusy-pastor.html

APPENDIX 2: AT A GLANCE

8 DECISIONS EVERY MAN SHOULD MAKE

1. **The King:** *To courageously lead some great cause in a way that others can follow.*
2. **The Lover:** *To give oneself to others for their benefit.*
3. **The Fighter:** *To vigorously fight for the right things.*
4. **The Jester:** *To enjoy life and keep having fun no matter how hard it gets.*
5. **The Artist:** *To make and enjoy beauty that is transcendent.*
6. **The Mourner:** *To embrace sorrow as a pathway to growth.*
7. **The Wizard:** *To humbly learn as much as possible and pass the same on to others.*
8. **The Mystic:** *To devote oneself to God and experience the things beyond.*

THE KING
Purpose*: To lead.*
Decision: *To courageously lead some great cause in a way that others can follow.*
Characterized by confidence; he is composed, able to confront, able to bear stress; he inspires others, is not easily offended, is sometimes lonely, and is able to serve.

Under-emphasis: The Abdicator
Characterized by complacency and irresponsibility; he plays the victim, complains, is a pushover, is non-confrontational; he avoids problems and is a brown-noser.

Over-emphasis: The Mogul
Characterized by overuse of authority and power; he is a controlling, intimidating, domineering tyrant.

THE LOVER
Purpose*: To love.*
Decision: *To give oneself to others for their benefit.*
Characterized by caring, serving, mercy, forbearance, and forgiveness; he imparts value, celebrates others, and adds to the atmosphere.

Under-emphasis: The Loner
Characterized by having no accountability and feeling nobody understands; he is impersonal and aloof.

Over-emphasis: The Hedonist
Characterized by thrill seeking, selfishness, and immorality; he is prone to addiction and gluttony.

THE FIGHTER
Purpose: *To battle.*
Decision: *To vigorously fight for the right things.*
Characterized by ferocity, passion, conviction, and fearlessness; he is sober, alert, inspiring, restrained, scarred, noble, and okay with losing.

Under-emphasis: The Coward
Characterized by laziness, complacency, and manipulation.

Over-emphasis: The Brute
Characterized by intimidation and irrationality; he is a bully.

THE JESTER
Purpose: *To play.*
Decision: *To enjoy life and keep having fun no matter how hard it gets.*
Characterized by fun, wonder, relaxation, and self-parody; he is naïve, oblivious, and carefree.

Under-emphasis: The Prude
Characterized by bitterness, a hard heart, and seriousness; he is smug, proud, emotionless, highbrow, and holds grudges.

Over-emphasis: The Fool
Characterized by decadence and addiction; he has no self-control, is an extremist, and seeks attention.

THE ARTIST
Purpose: *To create.*
Decision: *To make and enjoy beauty that is transcendent.*
Characterized by creativity, slowness, expression, substance, and depth; he is inspirational and content.

Under-emphasis: The Copycat
Characterized by trendiness, insecurity, pretentiousness, façade, and hype; he is a crowd-pleaser and a minion.

Over-emphasis: The Dreamer
Characterized by idealism, procrastination, self-importance, and exaggeration; he is manipulative, unfaithful, and disillusioned.

THE MOURNER
Purpose: *To grieve.*
Decision: *To embrace sorrow as a pathway to growth.*
Characterized by failure, depression, loss, and defeat. He is self-aware, transparent, and surrendered.

Under-emphasis: The Mannequin
Characterized by stubbornness and inflexibility; he is hardheaded and obstinate.

Over-emphasis: The Sulk
Characterized by narcissism and bellyaching; he is overly sensitive and easily offended.

THE WIZARD
Purpose: *To learn.*
Decision: *To humbly learn as much as possible and pass the same on to others.*
Characterized by humility, depth, and integrity; he is teachable, approachable, and willing to help others.

Under-emphasis: The Simpleton
Characterized by laziness, apathy, complacency; he is unwilling to change, irresponsible, hardheaded, and unambitious.

Over-emphasis: The Know-it-all
Characterized by arrogance and pride; he is aloof, snooty, and unapproachable.

THE MYSTIC
Purpose*: To transcend.*
Decision: *To devote oneself to God and experience the things beyond.*
Characterized by mystery, divinity, and depth; he is searching, risking, devoted, and virtuous.

Under-emphasis: The Degenerate
Characterized by immorality, debauchery, and waste; he is a godless reprobate.

Over-emphasis: The Hypocrite
Characterized by fakeness, two-sidedness, insincerity, and powerlessness; he is a master pretender.

ABOUT THE AUTHOR

Jeff Miller is a husband, father of four, songwriter, and clergyman. He and his wife Jennifer started Vineyard Community Church (vccaugusta.org) in 2001 in their living room with four people, a Bible, and a guitar. They continue to shepherd this thriving and eclectic family of believers which meets in a once-abandoned historic school building that Jeff helped restore. He spends his spare time running, building things, playing Scrabble, and generally avoiding social media.

Miller's writing and music can be found online on Amazon, iTunes, and other venues. He is available as a mentor, consultant, and conference or retreat speaker and can be reached at jeffreymiller5@yahoo.com.

Made in the USA
Columbia, SC
21 February 2020